Where There is A Will

God Does Not Have Favourites

VENANSIO AHABWE

WHERE THERE IS A WILL
God Does Not Have Favourites

Library of Congress Control Number: 2024942368
                       Paperback: 979-8-89306-065-2
                           eBook: 979-8-89306-066-9

Printed in the United States of America

CONTENTS

WHAT IS SUCCESS? 1

Success is the state a person attains after exerting an effort. It is a feeling of satisfaction and worth one finds in finding what one is looking for. It is when the person realises a dream. Success is not specific to some people and elusive of others.

SEEK WISDOM 5

Wisdom is God-given intelligence. It is the gift of judgement which a person gets naturally. Wisdom is often difficult, even impossible to account for. A person with wisdom might not be aware of his own endowment nor might he tell how it all comes about. Wisdom is simply a gift from God.

PLAN TO SUCCEED 11

"Always Plan ahead. It wasn't raining when Noah built the ark," once said Richard Cushing, a Cardinal-Priest and Archbishop of Boston.

SELF-AWARENESS MAKES IT EASY TO SUCCEED 17

A Proverb from the Bambara of Mali states, "No matter how long a tree trunk stays in water, it does not become a crocodile."

BECOME A RISK-TAKER 23

In Nigeria, they say, "When you seize a snake by its head, the rest of its body becomes a rope."

NOTHING IS IMPOSSIBLE 31

*"… if only you had faith the size of a mustard seed, you could tell that mountain to move from here… and (it would) obey." **(Matthew 17:20).***

I find it interesting that the meanest life, the poorest existence, is attributed to God's will... **Maya Angelou**

BOOK REVIEWS

"What sets Ahabwe's book apart is that it is localised to the Ugandan and African setting without losing the universal view that success can be attained by everyone who dares to exert themselves."

- *The Observer* newspaper, March 16, 2017.

https://observer.ug/lifestyle/51792-practical-advice-scented-with-scriptural-logic

"This book contains many quotes from scripture and applies it to real life circumstances so people looking to apply this thinking to their own lives would find this book helpful and enjoyable."

- Official review by OnlineBookClub.org, 12th February 2020.

https://forums.onlinebookclub.org/viewtopic.php?f=24&t=132646

"Irrespective of who you are, or what success means to you, this book is a must read."

- Review by Fortunate R. Akanyihayo, award-winning writer and teacher, 7 June 2022.

https://www.venansioahabwe.com/service/god-does-not-have-favourites

DEDICATION

Petero Kabunakuki and
Mariana Nyegirire
Humble but rich in faith and
integrity.

FOREWORD

How easy it is to become successful in life! No person or community was created to become a failure. Everything people need to live fulfilling lives was generously established within the physical, mental, emotional and spiritual set-up of every individual by the Creator. What man requires is to extract the inbuilt latent to attain success in life.

Success should not be viewed as an abstract element that is too distant and hard to realise. It should be understood as a simple and attainab.le condition by every human being. This is the reality you get after reading this book.

Where There Is A Will is an uplifting book. In it, you realise that God does not have favourites. The perceived differences in achievement are not a result of God's impartiality as there is nothing like that. Instead, they are a result of different mind-sets and approaches to human development by different persons and communities.

Western Europe and North America have traditionally been ranked as 'the developed world' but not every country in Europe or the Americas is so developed. Nor is every citizen in North America or Western Europe rich. Africa has, almost universally, been ranked as the least developed part of the globe but many studies find the happiest people in Africa. High suicide rates are found in rich countries. Failure to pay house mortgage or loss of job are major factors behind high suicide rates in Western Europe and North America. To many communities in Africa, a house (some would call a grass thatched hat) is built in one week by a large group of friends in the community. Belonging and social solidarity are successes that most value more.

In this book, Venansio Ahabwe shows that it does not matter somebody's status; they can achieve success if they pursue it with determination. It does not matter what roadblocks an individual or society might face in pursuit of success. People who experience success are not manufactured with special raw materials. Like everyone else, they are made of flesh, bones, blood and various other chemicals.

At the same time, success in the perspective of one person or society might not tally with what another regards as success. For a capitalist, success might mean the accumulation of material and monetary wealth while for a monk, it might mean a lifelong adherence to the vow of poverty. Success means different things to different people. To many, success resides in a set of values such as relationships with neighbours and God.

This, therefore, gives an interesting dimension to what we call 'success' and how we go about attaining it. It may be realised or defined in terms of people's motives in life. In my assessment, in this book, Mr Venansio Ahabwe challenges all of us to define our standard of success and pursue it irrespective of the hurdles along the way. Bravo.

Prof. Peter Freddie Ssengooba
Makerere University

INTRODUCTION

I was born in a large family with minimal resources. I did not go to school until the age of eleven when I went to the village church in the neighbourhood to receive basic Christian lessons before I could take Holy Communion. In a rare declaration that surprised the community, the local church teacher informed us that he would not recommend any child who was not in school to get the sacrament.

About fifty children had reported for instructions but only seven were in school. After separating school-goers from us, the daring catechist dismissed us from church. We could be readmitted only if we enrolled in school. I remember clearly what he said as he sacked us from the church course.

"A person who is not educated is also not fit to receive the body and blood of our Lord," he cried out.

The declaration was too strong, controversial and rather ironical. The catechist barely knew how to read and write in the local language because he had not gone beyond the lower primary school level. He could neither speak nor write a sentence in English. He did not have his own children in school. We did not know any of his relatives or neighbours who were educated. The Parish Priest had not instructed him to declare such a policy. It was the first and last time it became a requirement.

Nothing has shaped the course of my life like the catechist's action; at that time, I should have told him, "…this was not revealed to you by flesh and blood but by my Father in heaven," (Matthew 16:17).

My parents, whom we respectfully titled as Sebo and Nyabo, were not merely of advanced age and heavily saddled by a big family but they lived in an impoverished community where there was no incentive for taking children to school. Nevertheless, they sent me to a church-founded village school, a day after I had been dismissed from the religious lessons, so that I would be allowed to take Holy Communion. I could withdraw from school thereafter.

The school term ended before we had received Holy Communion and I was ranked the best in my class. This marked a turning point in my life as it motivated me to stay in school despite the poverty at home. In school, I was initiated to reading and writing while the church lessons centred on scriptural events and characters.

The Parish Priest distributed low cost bibles for children and encouraged us to read the sacred verses every day. I have since noted that all principles of success are imbued in the Bible. I also consider that I am a successful person for the big or small things I have accomplished. The Yoruba proverb soothes me: 'a chicken eats corn, drinks water and swallows little pebbles but still complains of having no teeth. If she had teeth, would she eat steel'?

In addition, I have learnt never to take anything for granted. While I can tell the story of my journey in education, I cannot understand fully the magic that flung me into school. I tend to attribute this miracle to the will of God. Things seem to me to have been very coherent as I moved from class to class; the Almighty must have plotted a track that I would only run along.

"We know that in everything, God works for the good of those...... whom he has called according to his plan" (Romans 8:28).

My school life was quite dramatic. The first book I carried to the church school was a sheet of paper, blank on one side but full of writings on the other. It was a letter my father had earlier received from a business partner, indicating the proceeds from coffee sales. Later as I joined secondary school, I was required to report with shoes. My father, Sebo, gave me his only pair, which was unmistakably worn out.

To raise school dues, Sebo started to look for casual jobs. Since he would never manage to raise a full term's sum, he always paid in small instalments. He would boost his meagre earnings by borrowing from kind companions to refund it with sales from the coffee harvests, which was a major source of income for the family.

On my part, I tilled in people's gardens during school holidays to earn money for my personal, basic needs. Sometimes, I gathered and sold firewood and bedding grass1[1]; made and sold mats; and later established a pineapple garden in the family backyard. Nyabo, my mother, was my bank and banker. I always handed every penny I got to her for safe custody.

Above all, Nyabo was very rich in faith and offered ceaseless prayers for me. On the outside, both my parents were poor but, at heart, they were abundantly rich. A Spanish proverb teaches: 'do not judge by appearances. A rich heart may be under a poor coat'.

Although the centre of all scripture is God and man's experiences with the Creator, the Bible contains people and events with pleasant episodes as well as moments of hardships, sometimes so severe. It is certain that all the joyful moments, including those following adversities, arise from God's magnanimity. Yet by creating man in His own image and furnishing him with complex faculties, God empowered humans to recognise His Will and translate it into personal and community success.

This book is a humble attempt to point out some biblical references that highlight the extent to which the Will of God can be recognised and applied in life. Scripture shows that God interacts with his creation according to a design: His Will. Individuals are expected to align their lives, decisions and actions with the Will of God.

God provides opportunities for every person and society to succeed. To make success real, one must be willing to succeed. One must have the will. 'The will' is the mental faculty by which one makes choices. All decisions and actions that people take should be based on the awareness of God's Will which must be the guide and cannot be thwarted.

David said to the people, "If it seems good to you and if it is the will of the Lord our God, let us…" (1 Chronicles 13:2).

The setbacks that a person may encounter in their pursuit of success must not deflate one's determination. An obstacle might be a mere test of one's determination to succeed; a strategy by which one is fortified to surmount greater challenges in life.

This book derives its title from the idiom, *"Where there is a will, there is a way"*, which suggests that if you truly want to do something, you will find a way to accomplish it, irrespective of any obstacles you meet.

---

1   Due to the rarity of decent beddings, people would knit sacks into mattresses which they filled carefully with soft grass.

As Don Moen sings, "God will make a way, where there seems to be no way! He works in ways we cannot see, He will make a way for you. He will make a way!"

Is there a place to which you want to go? Is it a property you want to acquire? Do you want to pursue a career? Do you want to belong to a community? Do you want to lead a life? It is by your own will that you can realise your dreams.

WHAT IS SUCCESS?

Success is the state a person attains after exerting an effort. It is a feeling of satisfaction and worth one finds in finding what one is looking for. It is when the person realises a dream. Success is not specific to some people and elusive of others.

In trying to interrogate the subject of 'success', I presented the question to several people from diverse professions, gender, age groups, education statuses and social ranks. I got as many dimensions about success as the people I asked.

A young man said, "Success is when you get married because there is a woman behind every successful man." He explained that he looked forward with anxiety to a day when he would get married as that would be the very time he would consider himself to have entered the ranks of successful men. Other responses from young people about the same question were: 'success is when you get a job'; 'it is when you are promoted at work'; 'when you get a salary increment'; 'when you build a house'; 'when you have a good car'; and 'when you get a degree'.

When this question was put to the married couples, a certain woman said that 'success is when you build a family house'. She explained that while she lived in the city with her husband and two children, her only prayer was for their family to acquire a private dwelling and move out of a rented flat. The day it happened, she said, she would have realised her greatest dream.

Other responses from married men and women were: 'success is when you are valued at home and at work'; 'it is when you have a stable family'; 'when you have bright children who are also disciplined'; 'when your children grow up as you desire'; 'when your tormenter faces a misfortune';

'when you have so much money that people admire you'; and 'when you are the first to acquire a particular item in the community'.

The descriptions above show that success does not have a single definition and it can be realised in different ways. A young man who considers that success is a state one attains after getting married clearly suggests that most people on earth are successful in life since they are married. It is, possibly, a few celibate priests, nuns and other exclusive persons that are not married.

The woman who relates success to a family house indirectly means that the world is primarily populated by successful beings because almost every person has an abode they call home. The family house may be located deep in the village. It may be built with rudimentary materials and in the most elementary fashion. As long as it is owned by the couple, it is 'a family house', therefore, an indicator of success.

Indeed, many of the scenarios mentioned - a job, a promotion, a good salary, a car, a house, a degree, a stable family, children and money - have been presented as instances of success.

Linda Seger2[2], the author of "*The Better Way to Win: Connecting not Competing for Success, and Spiritual Steps on the Road to Success: gaining the goal without losing your soul*" goes further to say that many people "define success by how their lives will be summed up at their funeral". Someone is interested in what the mourners would be talking about as his contribution on earth and how blessed they felt to have known him as a friend, neighbour or co-worker. Success is, therefore, not hard to attain. It is not the state of a person becoming an angel or a demigod. It is not about possessing what other people cannot have. Success is a state of being truly human.

In my interrogation, someone pointed out, "When a poor man gives an opinion but is ignored simply because he is poor, he will consider himself successful later when people realise that he was right after all."

A fisherman who has worked on the lake for twenty years might regard himself as successful by the mere fact that he has never drowned or run out of work all this time. There are countless men and women who are materially poor but psychologically successful. Success is emotional and can be almost totally experienced from within.

It is ironic, therefore, that people with high-sounding attainments like material wealth or academic expertise are essentially the only ones

---

2   http://www.fairfaxcountyeda.org/five-ways-define-success#sthash.njazN92y.dpuf - September 5, 2015.

considered as successful in life. In recognising such people, we deduce from their outward disposition as we cannot determine what they have at heart, whereas they might be inwardly tormented.

Someone may become 'successful in life' by stealing public resources. He knows, at heart, he is corrupt. He knows it is bad to be corrupt. He cannot boast about being the most corrupt individual. Therefore, corruption does not deliver psychological success. A man who amasses wealth through corruption and becomes famous is not successful in life.

When we use fraudulent means to derive 'successes', we become haunted celebrities. While success may be defined in many ways - material, spiritual or moral – it is not just what man can see, touch or hear but more about what one feels in the attainment of the intended desires.

Prestige, wealth, brilliance and development are indicators of success only if the person who has attained them believes that they are a result of sincere effort. Success is to know that you have achieved something, big or small, through honest means. As long as one is satisfied one has done their best, it does not matter if other people are dissatisfied.

"...... for power is perfect in weakness...... I am well content with weaknesses...... for when I am weak, then I am strong" (2 Corinthians 12:9-10).

SEEK WISDOM

Wisdom is God-given intelligence. It is the gift of judgement which a person gets naturally. Wisdom is often difficult, even impossible to account for. A person with wisdom might not be aware of his own endowment nor might he tell how it all comes about. Wisdom is simply a gift from God.

The second name of wisdom may be what we refer to as 'common sense'. Common sense has been described as the human attribute which is shared by all people: it is common to all. It is a person's capacity to recognise, understand and weigh things to make sound opinions and decisions.

As I grew up, Nyabo always amazed me with her degree of understanding of complex matters. Like many men and women in Kahengye village, she would appropriately estimate not only affairs in her control but also natural matters. Thinking back, I consider that my village was full of unschooled astronomers and weather experts.

Towards the end of a dry season, for example, Nyabo and her peers would till baked soils in preparation for the planting period. They could simply look at the trees bending to the force of the wind and declare the probable time for the rainy season to start. They would even announce the exact date of the first rainfall and it would happen.

There were times also when they would delay planting their crops during rainy days, asserting that it would stop raining in a few weeks or months and their crops might fail. Yet they would, at times, start sowing seeds of millet, beans, sorghum or peas in the course of an obviously dry spell, reasoning that the rains would commence shortly to aid the germination of the crops. They had a complex way of interpreting natural situations to arrive at appropriate conclusions. This was wisdom.

The women had a unique way of assessing pregnancies. Without the benefit of medical processes, they could infer, with bare eyes, that a girl or woman was pregnant. Depending on the month of her delivery, the women could predict, often accurately, the sex of the awaited new-born. Their predictions would essentially come true. This was wisdom too.

If a family member fell sick, an elderly man or woman would be consulted about the appropriate remedy. Very few cases were referred for medical treatment. Diagnosis was made by placing the back of a hand on the patient's body to gauge the temperatures and a relevant herbal concoction would be prepared to reverse the illness.

Some people's health would worsen, leading to death but this still happens in times of modern medical care. Almost all the pregnant women delivered babies from home, a practice that somehow persists. Yet, the only woman from my village who I remember to have died during childbirth died from a hospital.

In everything the elders did, they relied on natural intelligence. They did not go to school to learn about season cycles or how to combat ailments. This was a community of uneducated wise men and women who independently sought solutions to their problems with outstanding success. They were much wiser than their successors who, the higher they would go in education, the less they would utilise their brains to resolve the challenges in their lives.

Examining the concept of 'common sense', Robert Ingersoll, a nineteenth century politician and lecturer has said, "It is a thousand times better to have common sense without education than to have education without common sense."

Wisdom is the application of God-given intelligence that existed before the school systems were established. Education seems to subjugate a person to the intellect of other people who may have authored books or made proclamations on which learners are persuaded to rely for knowledge.

The best education should be one that does not impart knowledge to the learners but taps into and enhances their innate intelligence as human beings. There has been a mistaken belief that wisdom resides with famous people such as professors, kings, cardinals and merchants, who are largely reliant on the resources and knowledge of what they have read from other people's works. Little wonder that wars that have caused untold suffering and loss of life entirely always result from the thoughtless decisions and actions of these powerful characters.

People with little or no schooling have excelled in such fields as market vendors, basket makers, hunters, factory workers, fishermen and gardeners. They primarily use their natural intellect and a lot of the work they do sustains the world. However, they are less or never celebrated. Nyabo and her peers treasured and utilised their God-given wisdom.

German-born theoretical physicist, Albert Einstein, explains that the search for wisdom should be a lifetime undertaking. Wisdom is not a product of schooling but of the lifelong attempt to acquire it. It is the natural ability to understand things better than most other people. A person needs wisdom to live a fulfilled life. There is nothing a person with wisdom cannot do. Therefore, families, communities and nations would experience incredible development if people sought and gotten wisdom.

Solomon was still trying to find bearing in his office as king when God appeared to him at Gibeon and told him to make any request. Wisdom is the only thing he asked from God and the Lord was impressed. God said, "…since you have not asked for a long life but for wisdom and knowledge … therefore wisdom and knowledge will be given you. And I will also give you wealth, possessions and honour…" (2 Chronicles 1:11-12).

1 Kings 3:11-13 captures God's reply to Solomon a little differently. God said, "Since you have asked for this… I will do what you have asked…. Moreover, I will give you what you have not asked for… so that in your lifetime, you will have no equal….!"

Solomon's prayer fits well with the teaching of St James who says, "If any of you lacks wisdom, he should ask God, who gives generously to all without finding fault, and it will be given to him" (James 1:5).

If we are taking care of God's business as a priority, then He will take care of our business as well. We are to seek the things of God as a priority over the things of the world and this is what Solomon possibly had in mind when he prayed for wisdom. Clearly, a person with wisdom will always get success as a bonus. He who gets the wisdom of God gets everything.

Jesus Christ said, "…seek first his kingdom and his righteousness, and all these things will be given to you as well" (Matthew 6:33).

Wisdom has been ranked as one of the four cardinal virtues namely: prudence, justice, temperance and courage. These are a set of human qualities recognized, from ancient times and in Christian tradition, as the definitive standards for determining actual human decorum.

Casey Slide has also listed fifteen characteristics of a wise person. She says that wise people: 'educate themselves', 'are disciplined', 'admit their mistakes and learn from them'. They 'are patient', 'take instruction humbly', and 'can handle rejection and failure'. They 'know they can only control themselves', 'are guided by wisdom', 'know their priorities', and 'are trustworthy and steadfast'. They 'take calculated risks', 'make the most of their relationships', 'don't live beyond their means', 'don't pay full price' and 'don't squander money'. These truths mean that you do not need to look far away for opportunities, but rather to focus on the local options to register success. All success options are resident within an individual and the community.

The Akan people of West Africa say, "Wisdom is like fire.
People take it from others."

Wisdom is the only thing a person needs to live a fulfilled life

At the birth of Jesus Christ, three prominent men known as Magi turned up in Bethlehem with expensive gifts of gold, incense and myrrh for the baby. The Magi were referred to as wise men not only because they had the wealth and knowledge to travel and give admirable gifts but they were able to interpret mysteries of astronomy and spirituality. The star was a public secret as it appeared in the sky and was visible to everyone. That a star could appear in the sky was not an extraordinary occurrence as there were always stars in the sky at night.

As William Wordsworth says, "Wisdom is oft times nearer when we stoop than when we soar."

The Magi only required the wisdom of God to detect the unusual meaning from the star they followed. With God's regulation, they understood that a Divine King to adore was born, and they followed the star that heralded his birth. Once they were at Herod's palace, they asked, "Where is the one who has been born King of the Jews? We saw his star in the east and have come to worship him (Matthew 2:1-2).

Casey Slide may have presented the fifteen points about wisdom from a secular perspective but she does not contradict the Scripture at all. The Bible in fact says, "But the wisdom that comes from heaven is first of all pure; then peace-loving, considerate, submissive, full of mercy and good fruit, impartial and sincere" (James 3:17).

In another section, the Bible adds, "The mouth of the righteous man utters wisdom, and his tongue speaks what is just" (Psalms 37:30). Isaiah 11:1-2 proclaims the Redeemer of the earth who will be endowed with the Spirit of Wisdom. Indeed, the Holy Spirit imparts seven gifts, chief of which is wisdom. The Catholic Catechism describes 'wisdom' as the capacity to love spiritual things more than material ones.

It is because Jesus Christ radiated with wisdom that he was able to accomplish much more than anyone in human history; "Therefore, God elevated him to the place of highest honour and gave him the name above all other names" (Philippians 2:9).

God is the fountain of all wisdom and what human beings know and approve as such is, in fact, below the scale of God's wisdom, "For the foolishness of God is wiser than man's wisdom…" (Corinthians 1:25).

Scripture thus variously cites the fact that God is the sole source of true wisdom. "All wisdom comes from the Lord" (Sirachi 1:1). The fear of the Lord is the beginning of all wisdom (Proverbs 9:10).

As he commissioned his disciples, Jesus Christ warned that they would be tormented by their contemporaries in much the same way as wolves would treat the sheep. What they needed to overcome the persecution awaiting them was wisdom, "Behold, I send you forth as sheep in the midst of wolves; therefore be as wise as serpents…" (Matthew 10:16).

The world is probably becoming less and less enthusiastic about religion and the affairs of God generally. A man may argue that he possesses wisdom and yet he does not believe that God is responsible for his endowment. William Shakespeare would answer, "The fool doth think he is wise, but the wise knows himself to be a fool."

The more you distance yourself from God, the further away you move from the source of wisdom. Anyone who is ready to confront the world and all its trials needs the wisdom of God. Wisdom is the habit to act with the highest degree of adequacy under any conditions. It is a person's capacity to understand his circumstances and make good judgment that marks him out as a wise character.

English biologist, Thomas Henry Huxley, who became perhaps the finest comparative anatomist says, "Wisdom is the only medicine for suffering, crime, and all other woes of mankind."

PLAN TO SUCCEED

*"Always Plan ahead. It wasn't raining when Noah built the ark," once said
Richard Cushing, a Cardinal-Priest and Archbishop of Boston.*

Every person desires success. A student wants a successful school experience. A spouse desires a fruitful marriage life. An employee desires a rewarding work experience and to perform to the most remarkable highpoint. As a natural rule, people in all walks of life desire excellence in their respective areas of engagement.

The irony is that though our appetite for success is immense, the number of unsuccessful people exceeds that of the successful ones a thousand-fold. The problem is not because God wants some people to be frustrated and poor; He instead wants everyone to be successful in life. After creation, God blessed man and woman and conferred unto them authority to derive whatever they desired from the earth.

"God blessed them and said to them, 'Be fruitful and increase in number; fill the earth and subdue it. Rule over the fish of the sea and the birds of the air and over every living creature that moves on the ground.' Then God said, 'I give you every seed-bearing plant on the face of the whole earth and every tree that has fruit with seed in it. They will be yours for food" (Genesis 1:28-29).

We have since inherited the same resources given to our forefathers and are thus meant to put them to good use. With effective planning, the God-given resources are enough to bring prosperity to everyone; and success is not really a difficult state to attain.

Sebo grew up an orphan and did not get a chance to be baptised as a child. Therefore, he had to attend residential catechism lessons as an adolescent, after which he would receive the dual sacraments of baptism and confirmation in the Catholic Church. He joined the Christian course along with scores of other boys and girls from various villages.

He was a villager in all respects and very illiterate. However, he looked beyond baptism and confirmation right from the day he entered the parish. He had grown up under very difficult circumstances in the family and community, surviving on cultivation. At home, people would not think beyond the instincts of marriage, eating, rearing traditional animals and growing food crops for home consumption.

At the parish, Sebo noticed something different: the European priests led a better life than the local Christians. They had a car although they often walked to the outposts simply because of lack of community roads. He too wanted a car. They wore elegant shirts, jackets, trousers and shoes while the rest of the community members sported sheets of backcloth or scanty pieces of cloth and were barefooted all the time. He too wanted trousers, a shirt, shoes and a coat.

Sebo wanted everything that looked like a preserve for the European priests. He sensed that it was possible for a local African to attain whatever the Europeans had. From the day he set foot onto the parish grounds, he started to make strategies that would lead him out of personal and communal deprivation.

Curious as he was, he noticed that a number of local folks worked at the Mission as brick-makers, gardeners or carpenters. Some of them worked as builders since the priests were setting up churches in the outreach locations as well as schools, dormitories, offices and health centres. In all these, the participants earned some money.

He saw an opportunity to play a part in these projects and realised that he had to be exemplary to realise his dream. The priests encouraged the trainees to engage in agriculture, growing food on which they relied during their stay. Unless they were praying or studying, therefore, Sebo and his colleagues worked on the parish gardens, an experience most of them detested.

On his part, he always worked very hard and attracted the attention of the priests. They were impressed and, in the due course, brought him closer and assigned him extra tasks like slashing overgrown areas in the church premises, sweeping the church or piling bricks in one area. He slowly started to acquire building skills and, by the end of the course, Sebo was a trainee builder.

His classmates were nostalgic about returning to their homes and sighed with relief when they were baptised, confirmed and discharged but Sebo was already negotiating to remain at the parish as an apprentice. His request was granted and he was to be paid a stipend from this point.

Others were planning to get married and become respected men in their respective communities whereas Sebo's plan was to make money and become rich. It was an unwritten plan but materially clear in his mind. Soon, he was an expert at making bricks, building and plastering structures. He earned and saved money so carefully that by the time he got married, he was the envy of his peers. He was the most progressive young man in the entire neighbourhood. He could afford a coat, a pair of shoes, a shirt, a necktie and a cap.

Sebo was a man who wanted to succeed in life and he achieved success, step-by-step. After he had saved some money, he quit construction work and became a very successful coffee trader. As early as 1960, he owned a car and a cemented, iron-roofed house with painted doors and windows - the only one in the village. He had planned!

People who have succeeded in life are not branded necessarily with traces of pain or suffering resulting from tough effort. Rather, they are very likely to display a constant glamour of fulfilment. Success is not an impossible ideal. After all, successful persons do not drop from heaven; they are human beings like everyone else: our neighbours, peers, relatives, friends and other contemporaries. Success is what God desires for every person.

In the New Testament, Jesus said, "I have come that they may have life, and have it to the full" (John 10:10).

There are no exceptions to the promise given by Jesus Christ. However, success does not occur as an accident. The surest way to succeed is to have a clear idea in which you wish to succeed. The desire for success should be specific, not generic. It is a fact that one cannot excel at everything in any particular field, let alone in the broader arena of things. A great many people go through life, working hard to succeed but if you ask them to state, in precise terms, the specific area where they would wish to register success, they cannot say.

God gives blessings to all but some people squander their benefactions. Success comes by design, not by luck. A person who is passionate about success but is unable to detect God's favour and thus unsure what definite aspect he aims to succeed at only relies on luck. Yet when luck comes to a person who does not have a plan, it often ends as a missed opportunity. It is said that luck occurs when opportunity meets preparedness. You are prepared to benefit from your opportunities when you have a plan for your life. "Give me six hours to chop down a tree and I will spend the first four sharpening the axe," Abraham Lincoln, the sixteenth President of the United States of America.

A plan is the structural image of a future state of life

Planning is what defines a purposeful life. It is the centre of a focused personality. A plan makes it easier for you to set and meet personal targets. Planning brings personal joy as well as public respect. Jesus Christ provides a powerful answer to the question of planning.

"Do you build a house without first sitting down to count the cost and see if you have enough to complete it?...if you have laid the foundation and are not able to finish it, everyone will make fun of you ..." (Luke 14:28-30). The truth is that Jesus does not talk about building a physical house.

He uses a familiar analogy of constructing a home to relate it to any person. He broadly draws attention to the necessity of planning all the time in life. A person who does not plan walks along the highway of his life without any particular destination in mind. Such a person will not focus his attention and energy at any particular field of work.

You need a plan to serve as a structural illustration of your ultimate state of life arising from effort. Are you a student whose dream is to become a great statistician, celebrated engineer, a stirring artist, a prolific writer or an accomplished researcher? Reflect what you require to realise your dream and document it as a target.

In the same way, get a provisional idea of the family you desire before you can start one. Do you want a family to satisfy social demands? Are you looking for a happy family? Do you want a small or big family? It is up to you to construct the size, appearance, reputation or other state of your family, based on your interests and capabilities. In all this, do not forget to look out for God's Will. "Unless the Lord builds a house, the builders labour in vain"

(Psalms 127:1).

Scripture shows that for you to succeed, God should approve every plan you make. Your plan must be modelled on God's plan.

"Man's heart makes plans but it is Yahweh who answers…. Entrust all you do to Yahweh and your plans will be realised" (Proverbs 16:1-3).

Your every strategy must be guided by the Divine plan. All success springs from God, in whose image you were created. God's will for you is success. You were created for a Divine purpose. Prophet Jeremiah affirms that God's view is that you should achieve success in whatever you do.

"For I know the plans I have for you," declares the Lord, "plans to prosper you and not to harm you …" (Jeremiah 29:11).

You are on earth for a Divine purpose. You have the opportunity to detect God's purpose for you and pursue it. Perhaps He wants you to have a successful business; to be an effective teacher or steadfast physician; to practice productive agriculture; or to become a charming orator.

Whatever your goals are, reflect about God's plan for you and fit your personal plans into it. A plan helps you to assess your personal abilities and to define how much energy, time and other resources you may invest to meet your goals.

King Solomon gives instructive counsel, "Test the ground under your feet and your ways will be secure" (Proverbs 4:26).

Likewise, St. Paul instructs, "… by testing, you may discern what is the will of God, what is good and acceptable and perfect…" (Romans 12:2).

A key ingredient of success is patience. A plan that would bring durable outcomes does not necessarily yield instant results. You must be both patient and consistent right from the time of inception of your plan. You cannot reap from the garden on the day of sowing. Your duty is to look out for success all the time without giving up, and you will get your desired results at the appropriate time.

"There is time for everything … a time for planting, a time for uprooting …" (Ecclesiastes 3:1)

SELF-AWARENESS MAKES IT EASY TO SUCCEED

A Proverb from the Bambara of Mali states, "No matter how long a tree trunk stays in water, it does not become a crocodile."

Many people know very little about themselves or about the talents they are endowed with and, as a result, they unjustifiably experience failure. Others even attempt to deny or disguise their own attributes, forgetting that each person is unique and can never become someone else. The reasonable thing is to know and express your identity, which will help you to go far in life.

To register success, it is very important to have a clear opinion of who you are. This is known as self-awareness, which allows you to understand other people, how they perceive you as well as your attitude and responses to them. If you are self-aware, you hold an unbiased view of your own personality. You know your strengths, weaknesses, beliefs, emotions, and thoughts.

You can assess your abilities and pursue goals, which are in your means to achieve. Based on your self-assessment, you can tell where you need help from other people and thus are able to enlist their support. This helps you to apply yourself appropriately to pertinent matters in life.

Nyabo was a jolly mother who loved to joke and laugh with others. She was very peaceful, humble and, like Sebo, very generous. It is from her that I learned the quality of being at peace in whatever circumstances. A mother with an experience of fourteen sessions of birth pangs, Nyabo always beamed with contentment as she attended to the affairs of the home.

She was very successful in her own right: a mother of fourteen, a provider of all key family meals, a family counsellor, and the overall intercessor who never missed prayer.

It did not matter that she never went to school; her closest encounter with education was when she attended the catechism lessons. I always laughed each time Nyabo asked me how easy it was to construct letters and words. I would tell her that it was an effortless procedure. Sometimes I offered to teach her how to write but she never accepted.

One day, she joked, "I am happy I did not go to school! I would never have learnt how to write. How does one connect the various points to construct letters and words and sentences? It is a crazy process."

Nyabo was aware that she was not educated but understood that she could succeed in other things. Her husband spent most of his productive years pursuing business opportunities but she never complained about managing the family affairs like a single mother. She delivered almost all the babies unaided at home; she was often her own midwife and attendant. After delivering a baby, she would go out to prepare family meals.

She also breastfed and nourished all her children properly as none stunted. Above all, Nyabo sustained her marriage to death, in spite of numerous marital challenges she encountered. There can be no greater success for a family woman. Whereas education, which she lacked, is said to make people more enlightened, not many educated women would be able to sustain their marriages until death.

Throughout her marriage life, Nyabo established various gardens to feed the big family. She grew all crops such as bananas, cassava, potatoes, millet, beans, peas, pumpkins, yams, groundnuts, and tomatoes. It is safe to say that our family was a self-contained entity in terms of food. There was no need to buy foodstuffs from the market. Instead, Nyabo would generously donate to the families, which suffered food scarcity.

Overall, Nyabo was aware of her personal limitations but she did not descend into self-pity. She exploited her God-given faculties to succeed in life.

Timothy 4:16 says, "Keep a close watch on yourself and on the teaching. Persist in this, for by so doing you will save both yourself and your hearers."

Scripture further shows that reputable prophets were conscious of their human frailties when they took up the tasks God assigned them. Prophet

Isaiah, though appointed by God, assessed himself and acknowledged his personal flaws as well as those of his community. He was able to point out, with precision, the defect he knew about his life.

He told God that he was unfit for the assignment, "I am a man of unclean lips living among a people of unclean lips" (Isaiah 6:5).

Since he had the courage to acknowledge his weakness, Isaiah's frailty was mitigated and he was purified. The seraph took live coal with tongs and used it to touch his mouth, "...your guilt is taken away..." (Isaiah 6:7). Another prophet, Jeremiah was self-aware and did not pretend to merit God's favour. When God selected him, Jeremiah attempted to shy away from the task. He did not merely understand his limitations but he also had the audacity to declare the problem to God. In so doing, he earned the assurance.

"I do not know how to speak," he said, "I am young!" (Jeremiah 1:6).

God told him, "...you will go whatever be the mission I am entrusting you.... Do not be afraid... I will be with you..." (Jeremiah 1:7-8).

The interaction between Jeremiah and God, in this episode, shows that man has been endowed with an infinite capacity to register success beyond all expectations.

A similar thing can be said of Moses. When God asked him to coordinate the repatriation of the Israelites from Egypt, Moses was the least competent. What mattered was that he was conscious of his defective speech faculties. He knew where he required support and clearly pointed out the existing barrier.

Moses said, "...never have I been a fluent speaker ... I cannot find words to express what I want to say" (Exodus 4:10).

It is not surprising though that, later on, Moses accomplished the mission God assigned him. He primarily considered himself incompetent but God helped him to overcome the difficulty to such an extent that all the forty chapters of the book of Exodus seem to be a single story about the successes Moses registered.

The common element across the three characters mentioned above - Isaiah, Jeremiah and Moses - is that they were able to identify the imperfections in their lives and presented them to God. Accordingly, He resolved their worries and empowered them to perform their tasks with thrilling success. To acknowledge your limitations is the major step in overcoming them.

"The most fundamental aggression to ourselves, the most fundamental harm we can do to ourselves, is to remain ignorant by not having the courage and the respect to look at ourselves honestly and gently3."

Why did Zacchaeus climb up a sycamore tree? He was conscious of his personal strengths and weaknesses and he exploited both to improve his character. On one hand, he was rich, well-known and brave. On the other hand, he was very short, corrupt and hated. Aware that he was physically challenged, he sought the aid of a tree to improve his height.

"...he ran ahead and climbed.... From there, he would be able to see Jesus.... When Jesus came to the place, he looked up and said, 'Zacchaeus... I must stay at your house today'. Zacchaeus climbed down and received him joyfully" (Luke 19:3-6).

There is always a tree one can climb to improve the chances for success

Physical, social, economic or other challenges should not be cited to justify failure. As a Kenyan proverb goes, 'crawling on hands and knees has never prevented a baby from eventually walking upright'. There is always a tree one can climb to improve chances for success.

---

3   Adapted from Pema Chödrön's 'When Tings Fall Apart: Heart Advice for Difficult Times', a collection of talks.

Zacchaeus would have resorted to complaining about poor height! Short though he was, Zacchaeus got a clearer view of Jesus than his towering contemporaries. He even interacted with the Lord more intimately as he hosted him at his house. As a result, Zacchaeus got the opportunity to repent and amend his ways through almsgiving and compensation of all he had cheated.

"Zacchaeus spoke to Jesus, 'Half of what I own, Lord, I will give to the poor, and if I have cheated anyone, I will pay him back four times as much," (Luke 19:8).

This is clearly a case of taking advantage of every window of opportunity to improve oneself. Like Zacchaeus, you too can turn your weaknesses into strengths, if you are self-aware. God will remove the barriers which you can clearly identify in your life.

Your friends can support you to excel where you alone would not manage. Your employer will assign you proper tasks if you know where you have a niche. Your spouse will cooperate well if you know and share your peculiar interests and liabilities. As a student, your parents will provide for you if you can define your career dreams.

Jesus will change your water into wine. There must have been a lot of tension at the banquet of Canna when the servants and ushers noticed that they had run out of wine. They were sure the party was descending into a mess. Jesus learnt from his mother, the Virgin Mary, that there was a crisis.

He said to the servants, "Fill the jars with water…. Now draw some out and take it to the master of the banquet." When the master tested, the water had turned into wine (John 2:7-9).

What Jesus Christ did at Canna is precisely what God does for people who have the will and zeal to excel. A person who is determined to succeed in life will not abandon his mission when he encounters challenges. Instead, he will examine his circumstances and modify his character to skilfully operate within and exploit the existing conditions to derive the desired results.

You must grow up. You cannot remain childish and yet expect to gain the status of an adult. As an Arab proverb teaches, "You are not born a warrior; you become one."

Perhaps, the most compelling scripture about self-awareness is the story of the prodigal son. He reflected on his messy lifestyle and concluded that he deserved the suffering he faced. The only way to resolve his dilemma was to apologise to his father and request to be hired as a servant.

We note three important points from the parable. Firstly, the boy did not accept to stay in the sorry state forever. He decided to walk out of it. Secondly, he returned home to confess his mistake. Thirdly, he recognized that, since he had performed well during his wretched days as a pig herder, he would also excel as a casual labourer if only his father accepted him in that capacity.

He concluded that he was no longer fit to be regarded as a legitimate son and, therefore, would be privileged if his father could take him as a hired servant. The young man mustered the courage to assess himself. Based on his personal scrutiny, he took action and the story ends gloriously (Luke 15:11-32).

American award-winning writer, Elizabeth Gilbert has said, "We search for happiness everywhere, but we are like Tolstoy's fabled beggar who spent his life sitting on a pot of gold, under him the whole time. Your treasure--your perfection--is within you already. But to claim it, you must leave the busy commotion of the mind and abandon the desires of the ego and enter into the silence of the heart."

One African saying also puts it clearly: "When there is no enemy within, the enemies outside cannot hurt you."

You need to be sure of yourself so that nobody can mislead you. Jesus was able to overcome all the temptations because he clearly knew what he stood for.

The tempter told Jesus, "If you are the Son of God, tell this stone to turn into bread" (Luke 4:3).

Jesus rejected all the tempter's demands. He knew very well that he was the Son of God; and needed not carry out an experiment to prove His identity. When you are self-aware, you are able to hold on to your beliefs and to independently make decisions to modify your personality in terms of your thoughts, behaviour and actions, which is a key factor in achieving success.

According to Ngugi wa Thiong'o, "Being is one thing; becoming aware of it is a point of arrival by an awakened consciousness and this involves a journey" - adapted from *In the Name of the Mother: Reflections on Writers and Empire.*

BECOME A RISK-TAKER

In Nigeria, they say, "When you seize a snake by its head, the rest of its body becomes a rope."

In another version, the Congolese say, "He who looks for honey must have the courage to face the bees."

In the same way, a person who desires to succeed in life must be prepared to move out of the 'comfort zone' and take risks.

Nothing is more dangerous to a person than being a fainthearted character

People who take risks are able to conceive in their minds the conditions they desire to attain but for which they are prepared to pay the price. They are aware that there may be dangers along the way towards their desired achievements. However, they gain inspiration from the knowledge that the hurdles they might encounter in the process are surmountable.

Risk taking does not mean becoming reckless. It excludes violation of traffic rules, drug abuse, violence, or any other form of careless conduct. On the other hand, this text focuses on the necessary risks that a person may and should take to protect or improve the wellbeing of self and society. Such are the risks one takes to maintain, even enhance, one's dignity.

Sebo was either a hero or a coward. Women in Kahengye believed he was the latter while the men in the same village regarded him as the former. An incident in which Sebo fled from a dead snake that had been killed and thrown in the garden triggered the women's perception.

It was a popular practice for the community members to combine efforts and execute a task in a relatively shorter time than if a person or family had to accomplish it singlehandedly. Nyabo had thus invited some four women friends from the village to support her till and complete the field in one day so she could be able to plant beans within the season.

The women converged on the garden very early in the morning and had, by ten o'clock, done more work than the family could deliver in a full week. As they dag, the women were full of life. They chatted and laughed at the top of their voices. They seemed to derive vigour from the numerous stories and jokes they shared, some of which were just imaginary.

Suddenly, there was pandemonium as they threw away their hoes, screaming madly and running in different directions. While they tilled the land, one of them spotted a snake in a hole, dug by a mouse that must have already settled in the invader's stomach.

Terrified, all children scampered after their mothers. The reptile uncoiled from its hiding place and tended to wriggle away to safety when Kakazi, one of the women, returned with her hoe and landed a powerful blow onto the fleeing creature's head. She thrashed it severally until it lay on the ground, lifeless. Her colleagues too returned as she threw it at the edge of the garden. Everyone marvelled at Kakazi's daring character.

In a short time, Sebo arrived at the garden to appreciate the women's work that morning. He did not know they had encountered and killed a big snake. Hence, he got so close and was about to step on it when Nyabo alerted him.

When he looked down, Sebo saw the dead snake at his feet. He screamed, jumped and began to run, prompting all women and children to laugh wildly. Nyabo shouted out that the snake was dead. Hearing that, Sebo stopped a few metres away and returned to the scene, thoroughly embarrassed. The women branded him the most cowardly man they knew. However, men considered Sebo as one of the bravest men in Kahengye village. A large stream flowed through the area and often tempted hippos from the nearby Lake Nyabihoko to take refuge there if daylight broke before they went back to their habitat.

Hippos were feared because of their aggressive character, the harshness with which they were known for gobbling up victims and the grave destruction they visited on people's crops. One morning, someone noticed the hippo's footprints in the village and raised an alarm. It had invaded the village at night but hid in the nearby stream, leaving in its trails such damage that many villagers wept for their crops.

The whole village converged in the garden near the stream with spears, sharpened sticks and all manner of hunting weaponry. Sebo was among the group gathered by the bank of the stream when they spotted the hippo close by. There was an uproar as the crowd scuttled fearfully, some dropping their hunting tools. Sebo and two others stopped only a few metres away and returned to attack the beast.

As they took positions, the hippo seemed to make a slight movement and the men trembled again. By some impulse, Sebo flung a spear into the back of the hippo, so painfully that the monster charged out of the water in self-defence. Had it successfully pounced on him, Sebo would have been regarded as one who committed suicide.

However, more men advanced towards the hippo and randomly attacked it with spears, forcing it back into the stream. The assault went on until late in the afternoon. All this time, the hunters feared to get so close even as they noticed that it was already dead.

It was not until one man, Fabiano dared, stepped into the water and used a machete to cut a chunk of meat from the hippo's hip that they all followed suit. Every home had meat for dinner that day.

Scripture is awash with characters that took risks and emerged glorious. When Potiphar's wife demanded for sex, Joseph declined the request in spite of her insistence. She went ahead to grab him and force him into the immoral act but he abandoned his garment in her hands and ran away.

Joseph understood very well that he was taking a risk to embarrass his master's wife and, from the circumstances, he would face serious consequences. He was, nonetheless, willing to get any punishment other than betray his conscience. Indeed, the woman reported to her husband that Joseph had attempted to rape her but he fled from the scene and abandoned his garment in her hands when she yelled out for help.

The king was enraged and he imprisoned Joseph. However, the Lord protected him and, two years later, Joseph was released and immediately appointed a prime minister at the age of thirty (Genesis 39-41).

Similarly, Daniel 13:1-64 presents a moving story of Susanna, a strikingly beautiful wife of Joakim. One day, two lustful judges attempted to coerce her into having sex with them. Though wicked, the two elders had the power to condemn her to death.

Susanna was scared and helpless but she told them, "Yet it is better for me not to do it and fall into your power than to sin before the Lord."

Although they went ahead to sentence her to death, God sent the Holy Spirit onto Daniel, a young boy who challenged the elders' verdict, conducted a fresh inquiry into the matter and discovered that they were simply perpetrating injustice.

When Daniel established the facts against the elders, the whole assembly rose up and punished them in accordance with the Law of Moses. Susanna took the risk to reject the elders' demands and she emerged with her dignity intact.

To take a risk, you must be prepared to make sacrifices, to face pain and possibly to suffer total loss. This must have been Susanna's mind-set. A risk taker is able to see beyond the existing conditions and perceive the possible benefits that may arise from confronting a difficult situation, which weaker characters would not dare to face. It takes bravery to believe that even failure from a courageous decision is nobler than victory from a cowardly act.

Lailah Gifty Akita, a Ghanaian author has said, "Risks can lead to great victories or defeats. Even if you are defeated, the lesson will be valuable for the next stage of life."

Jesus Christ emphasises that success does not come on a silver platter, "…unless a grain of wheat falls to the ground and dies, it remains single. But if it dies, it produces many seeds" (John 12:24).

He adds, "…whoever would save his life will lose it, but whoever loses his life for my sake will find it…" (Matthew 16:25).

Moses was tending the sheep alone in the wilds at Horeb, the mountain of God, when he witnessed an eerie scene. A bush was on fire but it did not burn up. Instead of running away, he chose to move closer to observe the strange sight diligently. He had never heard of anyone who experienced such an incident so he was taking a risk to venture so close to the anomalous fire.

Nearer and nearer to the fire he went fearlessly and, in the process, encountered God who told him, "Do not come any closer. Take off your sandals…. I am the God of your father…. At this, Moses hid his face, because he was afraid to look at God" (Exodus 3:1-6).

Later on, Moses had to confront the Pharaoh with a message that the Israelites should be freed from the authority of the king's government. He was only a young herdsman, without any meaningful status to write home about.

Moses understood that the Israelites were mere slaves and strangers on the land, so it was risky to speak on their behalf. Moreover, the Pharaoh was a very oppressive king who reviled the Israelites and incited his people against them. The message from Moses provoked him to order that their suffering should be multiplied with more hard labour. In the end, Moses was able to lead the entire community out of slavery.

Someone might say that Moses succeeded in what he did because God contacted, sent and protected him. This is true. Equally, God directs everyone to attain success. Like Moses, you are expected to cast away all fearful tendencies, trust in God and pursue your dreams, no matter how risky the situation may appear. "And the day came when the risk to remain tight in a bud was more painful than the risk it took to blossom," Anais Nin, a Cuban-American author.

One evening, Jacob was alone after sending his family and possessions across the stream when a stern man challenged him to a wrestling fight. Jacob was not scared; he wrestled with the man till morning. When the man saw that he could not win the wrestling contest, he touched and injured the socket of Jacob's hip and demanded that he should be left to go. At Jacob's insistence, he found out that he had actually been wrestling with God, who blessed him saying, "Your name will no longer be Jacob, but Israel, because you have struggled with God and with humans and have overcome." Limping, Jacob left the scene as the sun rose above him (Genesis 32:22-31).

Other than wait to get a hip dislocation, Jacob would have escaped from the fight at the beginning of the fight. He did not, possibly because he trusted that he would eventually come out as the winner.

Many times, people miss opportunities to succeed when they flee from what may look as dangerous situations into what they regard as safe areas. They lose sight of the fact that nothing is more dangerous to an individual than a having a faint-hearted personality.

Abraham was able to get an heir when he was already very old. He should have been disturbed, nonetheless, when God told him to take his beloved son, Isaac, to the land of Moriah and offer him as a burnt offering. It was painful but God demanded it and Abraham obeyed.

"Abraham took the wood… laid it upon Isaac his son; and he took fire in his hand and a knife… and bound Isaac his son… Abraham stretched forth his hand, and took the knife to slay his son" (Genesis 22:6-10).

Abraham had such an abundant faith in God that he did not consider the possibility of dying without a successor as a grave risk to his lineage. Only God had a way of preserving Abraham's family. Indeed, God saved Isaac's life at the most critical point.

"'Abraham…. Now I know that you fear God, because you have not withheld from me your son, your only son.' Abraham looked behind and there in a thicket, he saw a ram caught by its horns. He went over and took the ram and sacrificed it as a burnt offering instead of his son" (Genesis 22:11-13).

A risk taken in obedience to God's Will is not a risk in the end; but an opportunity to achieve success beyond expectation.

Samuel 12 shows that King David was a crafty leader who slew a man, Uriah, to take a woman from him. Without fear, however, Prophet Nathan strongly criticized the king as a heartless man without a sense of justice. He delivered God's message to David so powerfully that the king instantly repented and never did such a thing again.

Nathan told David that he deserved death, "Why did you despise the word of the Lord by doing what is evil in his eyes? You struck down Uriah the Hittite with the sword and took his wife to be your own. You killed him with the sword of the Ammonites. Now, therefore, the sword will never depart from your house…"

Prophet Nathan's task would have sounded like the fable, 'Who will bell the cat'. Once upon a time, rats were concerned that a certain cat might exterminate them as it ate so many of their friends and relatives. The rats held a long meeting to discuss how to overcome the violent cat.

During the meeting, the rats resolved, by popular acclamation, to look for the cat and tie a bell around its neck so that whenever the bell would tinkle, they would tell where the cat would be and avoid it. When it came to selecting the rat that would tie the bell to the cat, none came forward. Whereas they had a great idea, they did not try to implement it. They considered that any rat that attempted to bell the cat would end up as its meal. As a result, the problem remained and the cat kept hunting them, anyway. Who knows, the rats might have found the cat asleep and tied the bell, but none of them attempted the assignment as each feared for its life! Lions are ranked as man-eaters; animals that relish human flesh as a part of their natural diet. Other such animals include tigers, leopards, and crocodiles. I recollect from my early school studies that the Man Eaters of Tsavo were two notorious lions which disrupted the construction of the Kenya-Uganda Railway as they ate some one hundred thirty-five workers during the building of a bridge over River Tsavo in 1898.

The Bible shows, however, that while he was tending his father's sheep, David could rescue lambs from lions and bears and strangled the aggressive animals.

He told Saul, "Your servant has killed both the lion and the bear…" (1 Samuel 17:36).

Another young man who killed a lion was Samson, "Then Samson went down to Timnah…… suddenly a young lion came roaring towards him…… he tore the lion apart with his bare hands…" (Judges 14:5-6).

A lot of the time, God is available to enable you accomplish an impossible task but the only thing He requires of you is to take a daring step. It has been stated that risk is that precarious link between success and failure; between hope and despair; between life and death.

NOTHING IS IMPOSSIBLE

*"... if only you had faith the size of a mustard seed, you could tell that mountain to move from here... and (it would) obey." **(Matthew 17:20).***

Nyabo saw me dying! She did not know how to announce my death. She paced the room restively like a puzzled mouse. The family was going to carry out another child's funeral in less than five years and the sixth since Sebo and Nyabo got married. My brother, Alfonse, was the most recent case who had died within a week of his illness.

It was the beginning of the new school term and I had just spent two weeks of my second term in Primary Four when, by surprise, I was attacked by an illness. My ailment was not clear since it was never diagnosed. If someone fell sick, the normal practice in the community was to exempt the patient from work, keep them in the house, inform the neighbours about the problem and apply herbs and other traditional potions for treatment. Very few people would take their patients for medical attention. In my case, I was unable to continue with studies and, therefore, had to stay at home until I could recover. I had been bedridden for three weeks and kept on herbal treatment all this time. Gradually, my health deteriorated and Nyabo became very concerned.

On her part, the risk of losing another child was real and painful, so she wanted to do something to avert it. She had hosted me in her womb for nine months, weathered the pangs of labour at my birth, breastfed me as a baby, given me full care as an infant and prayed that I would grow into productive adulthood. To see me dying at such a tender age was a very hurting spectacle.

She later was able to give an account of what happened on that troublesome day. She had returned from the garden, entered my bedroom and found me open-mouthed and motionless. She was dumbstruck. She was alone in the house and had to bear the situation by herself. She got closer, touched my chest and felt a delicate heartbeat.

On the other hand, my body was so hot that the bed was almost catching fire. Nyabo believed that it was the heat that was suffocating me. She dragged me out of the bed, into the compound and rested me on the grass in a tree shade. On closer examination, she noticed what looked like a swollen vein on my forehead which she concluded was the source of the problem.

She had to save her lastborn. She dashed into the house and collected a harvesting knife which was the first sharp item she came across. Nyabo wanted to carry out a surgery. She knelt by my side, placed the sharp point of the knife to the strained vein and cut deep into the skin.

Things turned out differently. Blood gushed out of the wound uncontrollably; it splashed like water rushing from a broken pipe. This was a quicker way of ending my life as I was running out blood and would die in a matter of minutes. Nyabo regretted what she had done but could not sit and watch helplessly.

She hurried into the banana plantation and picked all sorts of herbs. She crushed them with her hands, pressed them on the wound and tied them firmly using an old cloth she used as a headscarf. She had controlled the bleeding as the volume of blood loss lessened.

Amidst all this, I still lay motionless and, when she checked again, she detected no heartbeat. She was sure she had drawn the last nail in my coffin and she would be accused of causing or quickening my death. It would not be considered a natural death.

Nyabo told herself, "I am guilty. I have killed my son. Why did I cut that vein?"

She carried 'my body' back to the bedroom as she prepared to break the sad news to other family members as well as neighbours and relatives. What she had feared had happened! She again paced around the house pensively, a rosary in her hand as she recited numerous prayers. She called on Jesus Christ, the Virgin Mary, the Holy Spirit, the Guardian Angels, the Holy Trinity, and all the Saints to receive my soul.

A few minutes later, Nyabo returned to my bedroom to arrange everything so that mourners would find an organised setting. She did not believe what she saw. My eyes were blinking slowly and I seemed to breathe. She had not anticipated such a miracle. She was even more confused. Should she hold the patient by her chest? Should she give a drink?

Nyabo sat down and surrendered the situation to the Almighty. Hours, days and weeks passed. My health improved. I returned to school the following term. Twenty-five years later, she went to the next world. In earthly terms, her prayer had been answered already: I had become the productive adult, able to make her old age enjoyable.

The Bible presents a story of a man whose son was born epileptic. In search of Divine therapy, the man prayed to Jesus Christ, "If you can do anything, take pity on us and help us."

Jesus did not like the man's partial conviction about the possibility of his son's healing, so he replied, "Why do you say 'if you can'? All things are possible for one who believes" (Mark 9:23).

In a sense, the man needed to fortify his petition with faith and wait for the results. Many people put a lot of effort to achieve their goals in life but fail to accompany their labour with hope. If we all did, no one would ever die with unfulfilled dreams.

In yet another incident, the disciples tried and failed to drive out a demon from an epileptic boy simply because they lacked faith. A person with faith can move mountains. When Jesus intervened, he ejected the demon with ease. They were amazed and decided to ask him why it had been impossible for them to expel the demon.

Jesus told them about the power of faith, "… if only you had faith the size of a mustard seed, you could tell that mountain to move from here… and (it would) obey. Nothing would be impossible for you" (Matthew 17:20).

W.E.B. Du Bois, who is said to be the first African-American to earn a doctorate says, "There is, in this world, no such force as the force of a person determined to rise. The human soul cannot be permanently chained."

Any person facing difficult conditions, therefore, ought to remember that hard times can only persist if the person involved does not make deliberate effort to arrest the situation. There is no condition that is permanently difficult.

All of us can register success if we want it. You can achieve anything if you put your mind and effort to it. A community can register impressive development if its members decide to work hard for it. A country grows when the citizens take serious decisions, become determined and inspired and go out to attain progress.

Social or personal advancement should not be hindered by simple limitations such as local traditions, physical deficiencies, financial inadequacies or other contingent shortcomings. Two people may experience the same wretched conditions. The difference exists when one strives hard and consistently to overcome the challenges at hand, while another one surrenders to the prevailing inferior state of affairs.

In education, two students may be attending a 'third class school' together, yet one could manage to score amazing grades whereas another scores poor marks and goes ahead to attribute the poor performance to the sordid state of the same school.

You meet a disabled beggar in one corner of the town and a disabled entrepreneur in another corner. In marriage, you can find a joyful partner of a reckless spouse in one home and miserable partner of a decent spouse in another.

With God, nothing is impossible

Your level of success in any field largely accrues from your own will. The problem arises when a person lacks confidence and therefore tries to minimise his own capacity to achieve success.

Genesis 12:1 shows that when God told him to migrate to a strange land, Abram saw it as a blessed opportunity, obeyed God's word and never looked back. It was obviously a tough decision to leave his property, relatives and other social trappings but Abram had the courage to take action. Listening to the inner self, he dreamt of a brighter future in terms of a great nation and thus followed his mind. Perhaps, you too have heard a Divine voice urging you to take tough decisions. Your task is to adhere to the voice of God who inspires everyone to be ambitious and blesses the effort of people who pursue success.

Someone would have worried about the evident risks of an old man starting from scratch in an unfamiliar setting but Abram did not. In the pursuit of a higher good, therefore, obstacles and limitations mean nothing. Ronald E. Osborn, the author of *Death Before the Fall* counsels, "Undertake something that is difficult; it will do you good. Unless you try to do something beyond what you have already mastered, you will never grow."

What if you meet frustrations as you pursue your dreams? Do not give up still. Abraham did not give up although he was of advanced age. For a long time, he did not get what God had promised him but his faith never diminished.

At the age of 100, he did not have an heir and his wife, Sarah, was similarly so old. The couple's reproductive ability was 'past expiry date' but God's angel told them to expect a son within a year. On learning about the possibility of a son's birth, Abraham and Sarah were extremely amused.

Sarah was not excited and instead doubted saying, "… I am old and worn and my husband is an old man". The Angel assured them with an answer, "Is there anything that is impossible for God?" (Genesis 18:14).

Later on, God's promise was fulfilled and Abraham's faith was rewarded when Isaac was born as predicted. God is always available to bless your effort if you take courage to pursue success against all odds. You need confidence and determination, capped by the grace of God, to register success in any situation.

In David's song of deliverance, he chants, "In your strength I can crush an army; with my God I can climb any wall" (2 Samuel 22:30).

How can a woman become pregnant without a man, sex or any form of insemination? Mary was a virgin and unmarried. However, Angel Gabriel declared that she would become pregnant. Mary initially did not understand the Angel's message. She was troubled greatly by the Angel's pronouncement.

However, the Angel provided very instructive counsel, "With God, nothing is impossible" (Luke 1:37).

Why did Jesus Christ not give up during the Gethsemane episode? It was here that he faced untold grief as he thought about his looming death. It was obvious that danger was brewing up for him. However, he did not surrender to despair.

Jesus Christ found assurance in the unfailing power of God which he acknowledged in his penultimate prayer, "Abba, Father, all things are possible for you..." (Mark 14:36).

If ever you should find bumps and corners on the road that leads to success, remember that God has a solution to every difficult situation, no matter how gloomy it may seem. With God in your company, therefore, you should never give up on your dreams.

At Bethany, Jesus Christ taught his disciples about the force of faith or willpower. They had asked him how he managed to curse a fig tree and it dried up in one day.

Jesus told them, "Whatever you ask in prayer, believe that you have received it and it shall be done for you" (Mark 11:24).

The basic requirement is to examine yourself and understand the exact favour you want from God. If you offer a petition to God after serious reflection, you are eligible to obtain a favourable, Divine answer. It then remains a matter of when and how, not if, you are going to get your prayers answered. Effective prayer is prayer made in faith.

In his prayer, Jeremiah proclaims the boundless power of God, "Ah, Lord Yahweh, you have made the heavens and the earth with your great power and mighty deeds. Nothing is impossible for you" (Jeremiah 32:17). Compared to the entire creation that God put into place, your personal needs and, indeed those of your community or family are very easy for Him to deliver. There is a solution to every hopeless condition.

During the wedding at Canna, "… they had run out of wine… Jesus said to the servants, 'Fill the jars with water….' When the steward tasted the water, it had become wine…" (John 2:3-10).

Jesus' encounter with the rich young man also highlights everyone's limitless ability to excel. The disciples became nervous when Jesus told the rich man that although he kept all the commandments, he also needed to sell all his property and give the proceeds to the poor.

They felt that this was a harsh requirement and wondered, "Who then can be saved?" Jesus told them, "For human beings, it is impossible, but for God, all things are possible" (Matthew 19:25-26). Success in life often appears wrapped in hostile conditions,

but one must never get disheartened: "For with God, nothing shall be impossible" (Luke 1:37)

NEVER GIVE UP

I have walked that long road to freedom. I have tried not to falter; I have made missteps along the way. But I have discovered the secret that after climbing a great hill, one only finds that there are many more hills to climb"-
Nelson Mandela in A Long Walk to Freedom.

Mandela's declaration denotes that life consists of a series of endless, vexing obligations. To give up is to stop to live. A spouse must constantly cater for the partner's needs, no matter how bothersome. A student must persistently attend lessons and academic preps regardless of the resultant headache. A farmer must plant and care for his crops from season to season irrespective of the unfavourable weather. A shopkeeper must open for customers and replenish the stock constantly, notwithstanding the fluctuations in client flow. A priest must preach and minister to his flock continually, even though his message often goes unheeded. As a coffee trader, Sebo became relatively rich, probably the richest in the neighbourhood. He acquired a sizeable chunk of land and, in later days, started donating fragments of it to landless immigrants. His major regret in life was that he had never gone to school since he only acquired miserable reading and writing skills during his catechism course.

It always saddened him that he could not speak English, which was quite easy for the people who looked to him for support such as school teachers, agricultural extension workers and community health inspectors. Sebo attempted to compensate for his lack of education by offering financial support to both the church and neighbouring schools, in addition to sponsoring a few boys' education.

The missionaries had set up schools in the community and encouraged parents to send in their children but many did not see the value of investing in education. They felt that it would cause them a lot of inconvenience as they were used to a hassle-free lifestyle.

Wherever there was a school, parents had a duty to set up some of the basic facilities such as pit latrines and classrooms. Yet many did not want the bother of attending school meetings, paying school fees and participating in building such school structures. Whereas he had missed going to school at his time, Sebo wanted it for others and looked forward to successfully giving this golden chance to his children or other beneficiaries. Sadly, his dreams were shattered. By the time he attained the age of fifty-five, his life took an unpleasant twist. He had a big family of fourteen children, all of whom had dropped out of school, apart from two boys who were yet to join school.

The big family also faced an acute shortage of food and other necessities. His businesses had collapsed as the coffee prices plummeted. He had sold most of his animals, part of his land as well as commercial buildings in Mbarara and Rukungiri towns, hopping to revive his business fortunes but all in vain.

Sebo retreated to the village to face the harsh realities of peasant life, ruled by daily drinking of the local brew, *tonto*. He gave up the culture of wearing shoes and suits often and started walking barefooted like everyone else in the community. It was a dog's life; he had returned to the undesirable state of poverty from which he had intended to run away when he stayed at the parish to work for money while his peers returned to the village after completing the catechism course.

Ironically, some of the neighbours liked Sebo's new peasant status. Many had accused him of pride and arrogance during his prosperous days. Apparently, he would give unsolicited advice to some community members about how they could achieve development like him. They construed his advice as bragging and a way of despising them.

As his fortunes had taken a nosedive, therefore, the people were happy to remind him how he had squandered his wealth and thus he was nothing but 'a prodigal son'. The severe environment in which Sebo ended up should have shattered him.

None of his grownup offspring could rescue the situation as they all had absconded from school before completing the primary school cycle.

It was almost too clear that he would never derive redemption from the education of his children or of other dependants. Neighbours believed that it was easier for a camel to go through the nose of a needle than anyone from their community to succeed in school.

It was then that I was enrolled forcibly at the church school and, fast forward, I was to do my primary leaving examinations in a few years. Luckily, I scored an excellent grade and was admitted to Muntuyera High School, to the surprise of my family and our neighbours. However, the dire economic situation at home would not favour my good academic scores.

In addition, Sebo's friends would advise him to ignore my performance and simply tell me to stay at home and get married like most of my peers were doing. What everyone knew was that every boy would eventually need a wife whether he was educated or not. One of the neighbours told his own son to use the family cows to marry a wife other than selling them to raise school dues without the guarantee that there would be cows in future if he delayed marriage.

Sebo was told how he was already too old to benefit from my education if at all I completed school several years later. Like Job, however, Sebo did not give up. At about sixty-five years of age, he was also considered too old to successfully meet the demands of a secondary school student.

Someone told him that it was not possible to get from the lastborn what he had not achieved from his other thirteen children, most of whom had grown up when he was wealthy. Yet he had dreamt of an educated child and a decent life in old age, which he had not yet achieved.

As an Ivorian proverb teaches, "Until the snake is dead, do not drop the stick." Sebo gave a deaf ear to the wild discouragements from doomsayers.

Like Abraham, he was prepared to start life all-over again. He went back to the job market as a builder but his bargaining power had gone down since he was aged and had been out of practice for more than three decades. To discourage him from asking for jobs, clients always offered very little pay but Sebo was desperate for money and did not mind being exploited.

He withdrew from boozing in order to save money for my school dues. He sent me to Muntuyera High School and successfully negotiated to pay school dues in small portions every term. During this time, he became a perpetual borrower, but he was prepared and happy to become a debtor all his life as long as I remained in secondary school. On numerous occasions, he walked more than thirty kilometers to the school, six times in one term, to pay the fees in instalments.

In their late seventies and early eighties, the family of Sebo and Nyabo had regained glory. The sweat of their old age was rewarded. They had almost everything that an old man and woman required to lead a decent life in the village. A car was always at hand as well funds for urgent medical care. Their house was revamped seriously to become the best in the neighbourhood again.

Clearly, Sebo had lost his material wealth but not his mind-set to prosper and always asked, "Can anything ever separate us from Christ's love? (Romans 8:35).

Not even broken bridges should block your journey to success

Jesus stressed the importance of perseverance. He said that if you have a friend and you knock at his door for assistance late at night, he might not open to assist you at first. If you are in serious need of help, however, you must not give up your appeal.

Knock more and more, "…even though he will not get up and attend to you because you are a friend, yet he will get up because you are a nuisance to him…" (Luke 11:5-8).

There is another scriptural story of a widow that seriously needed justice. When she took her case to the judge, he totally ignored her. The widow, however, did not give up her request to the judge to intervene in her case. When she persisted with petitions for justice, the judge got tired and sorted her case to save himself from further inconvenience (Luke 18:2-5).

Success is registered rarely at a single click of a button. In a majority of cases, success is a product of endless pressing of buttons; some right, some wrong. Tireless attempts at tasks results into learning new lessons each time and what follows ultimately is to become innovative, which also translates into desirable success.

Sir Winston Leonard Spencer-Churchill, a Prime Minister of the United Kingdom (1940-1945/1951-1955), once said, "Success is going from failure to failure without losing your enthusiasm."

In a speech to new graduates at Wellesley College in 1997, Oprah Winfrey also pointed out, "Turn your wounds into wisdom. You will be wounded many times in your life. You'll make mistakes. Some people will call them failures but I have learned that failure is really God's way of saying, 'Excuse me, you're moving in the wrong direction.'"

The bumps that you experience along the road to success are not pointers that the highway has been totally closed. They are simple reminders that you should not go to asleep as you drive, lest you crash in an accident. A great many people though easily surrender to despair and abandon their dreams when they are so close to success that they only need to take a single step to attain victory.

In the words of Napoleon Bonaparte, a revolutionary French Emperor, "Victory belongs to the most persevering."

There was a woman who suffered from severe bleeding for twelve years. She always looked everywhere for cure and used up all her property to sort her treatment bills. She did not give up though. When she came across Jesus, she touched his clothing, resulting into instant cure (Luke 8:24-29).

Twelve years is not a short time but the woman did not stop seeking a remedy for her condition. When you set your mind and energy on something, nothing should stand in your way to attain it. Barriers will surely crop up, including delay, sabotage, exhaustion, competition, or misfortune. Yet, these are not real barriers; they are mere figments of your imagination. If you do not create a comfortable zone in your mind for the worries to thrive, you will realise your dreams or goals. The road to success tends to be rich with parking spaces; thus many people are easily tempted to park their automobiles along. Others who are bound to succeed may see these spaces but they know they can only pull the car off the road after the trip is done.

A man was sick for thirty-eight years and stayed at the pool but had no opportunity to leap into the water first to be cured. In spite of this challenge, the man did not give up until Jesus found him at the pool and healed him.

"When Jesus saw him lying there and learned that he had been in this condition for a long time.... Then Jesus told him, 'Get up! Pick your mat and walk.' At once the man was cured; he picked up his mat and walked" (John 5:6-9).

Supposing the man had got frustrated and left the scene of healing, he would never have encountered Jesus. He would have remained sick or died. When you are pursuing a cause, you should never surrender to frustration or disappointment. Churchill again emphasises, "If you are going through hell, keep going."

One of the strongest people in the Bible, Samson, identified a woman of his love (Judges 14:1). In pursuing his dream, he encountered two major challenges which he nonetheless faced squarely. First, when he was going to Timmah to talk to his branded woman, a lion got in his way. Instead of retreating, he grabbed and tore it into pieces (Judges 14:6).

The second challenge is that Samson's father strongly opposed Samson's intention to marry a Philistine. Samson was not discouraged though. He remained firm in his pursuit of his loved woman and, in the end, his father supported the marriage.

From conception, God had revealed Samson's mission to his parents, "He shall begin the liberation of the Israelites from the Philistine oppression (Judges 13:5).

When Samson grew up, however, the Philistines seized him, gouged out his eyes, imprisoned him and subjected him to harsh labour (Judges 16:21-22). They brought him to their council, as an amusement character, and made fun of him.

In the due course, Samson "...called on Yahweh and exclaimed, 'Lord Yahweh, remember me...'". He pulled down the pillars and the council house fell upon the chiefs and the entire gathering. Ultimately, Samson accomplished his mission (Judges 16:28-30).

The circumstances leading to Samson's final triumph were gravely torturous and demoralising to him as a person but also to his relatives, friends and well-wishers. However, he persisted and achieved his mission. Where God is involved, everything is possible (Luke 1:37).

The people who carried a sick man to Jesus found that there was no space for them to access the Lord. He was inside the house and, worse still, the entire compound was overcrowded. They should have given up and returned the sick man home to die or they would have waited for Jesus outside the building. However, they did not want to gamble with the man's life.

"They could not get space because of the crowd; they removed part of the roof till they got the paralytic man to Jesus… and he was healed" (Mark 2:4-5).

Alchemist Paulo Coelho says, "The secret of life, though, is to fall seven times and to get up eight times."

Actually, Coelho means that when you remain committed to succeed, all the roadblocks to your efforts will eventually disappear and, at your ultimate attempt, it will be a smooth ride.

Similarly, Francis Bacon (1561-1626) an English philosopher, statesman, jurist and author says, "Fortune is like a market where, many times, if you can stay a little, the price will fall."

St Paul also says, "Let us not become weary in doing good, for at the proper time we will reap a harvest if we do not give up" (Galatians 6:9).

The Scripture further states, "Blessed is the man who remains steadfast under trial…." (James 1:12).

We all have equal chances to succeed in life. It is natural, however, that we meet numerous challenges which may discourage some people from moving forward. Such people may wish to wait until they are sure they will not pay any price in terms of risks, competition, or tiredness. All success demands a price and to give up is to refuse to pay.

In his book, *How to Win Friends and Influence People,* Dale Carnage says, "If you believe in what you are doing, then let nothing hold you up in your work. Much of the best work of the world has been done against seeming impossibilities. The thing is to get the work done."

HARD WORK BRINGS BLESSINGS

An African Proverb proclaims, "Success is a set of ladders which you cannot climb with your hands in the pockets."

Lazy people invite poverty onto themselves. Poverty is a very sad status whereby the affected persons live in multiple deprivation and utter lack of basic requirements of life. It is total misery.

King Solomon screams, "How long, you idler, are you going to lie around? When do you intend to rise from your sleep? A little sleep, a little drowsiness and your laziness creeps upon you and then, like a tramp, poverty comes to bring misery like a vagabond" (Proverbs 6:9-11).

Insects should be everyone's role models in matters of work. They spend their full lives performing productive work, and are able to invest for the future, yet they do not possess a conscience like humans. Learning from them, therefore, a human being should be in a better position to appreciate the value of working hard, beyond the perspective of an insect. Small as they are, insects are never tired of working and the Scripture recognises them.

"You idler, go to the ant, watch her ways…. She secures food in summer and stores up provisions during harvest time" (Proverbs 6:6-8).

An unwritten agreement existed between Sebo and me as I pursued my education. Sebo was resource constrained and could only raise money for school fees while I catered for other basic scholastic items such as stationery, extra school wear, soap, sandals, or club fees.

As a result, I had to look for ways of supplementing whatever Sebo provided. During my primary school time, I was privileged to participate in handiwork competitions and perfected my skills in making mats out of papyrus reeds and palm leaves, moulding hoe handles, carving stools, decorating calabashes and trimming compound plants.

A dung beetle can roll a dung ball 10 times its weight to have it for food

In part, handiwork was an academic activity and participants earned marks based on how skilfully they crafted their articles. Besides, it was a source of income and, therefore, a way of equipping learners with moneymaking skills. The teachers would fix a price for each student's product and organise an open market within the school to which members of the public were invited to buy.

We all would be present to see how much the buyers were paying for our items. Some articles fetched higher prices than the rest owing to the fineness with which their makers finalised them. A pretty piece would generate a lot of haggling by different bidders and this was always uplifting to the student responsible for its production.

During the school holidays, I would apply my handicraft skills to make personal money since all the materials needed to make most of the handiwork items were free of charge. I would work on the family gardens together with other family members for most of the day and thereafter dedicated evening time to make mats. I was so committed that I could work until night time, especially during the period of the full moon.

I still utilised my handiwork skills when I joined secondary school since I needed money more than during the primary school days. The problem was that production of handiwork articles tended to be relatively long, yet they fetched low prices.

Therefore, I had to make some more money through vending sugarcanes, collecting and selling firewood, brewing alcohol and working as a casual labourer in neighbours' plantations and building sites. Newly married men also needed bedding grass. I would be at hand to collect and sort the grass carefully for sale.

Many of my peers who had dropped out of school had married young girls before they travelled to various places to do menial jobs like wheelbarrow pushing, brickmaking, stone quarrying, street hawking or car washing. They would send money to their young wives who would use it to establish family gardens. During the holidays, I would be hired to do such work. Some people would be surprised that I could go that far.

My objective was to avoid being a burden to my parents by asking for simple things and to ensure that I procured the very basics required for a meaningful school life. I needed to buy a cluster of sweet bananas at least three times in a week as well as acquire simple items like soap, toothpaste, a jacket, shoe polish or pants. If I had to write a love letter, like other boys, I had to buy an envelope and postal stamps as well as hankies or sweets to enclose.

Hard work is the basis of human survival, and a person who is not willing to work hard degrades his humanness. Every person has a duty to work to prove the relevance of his existence on earth and to sustain his life. Laziness breeds poverty and begging and the victim is not able to become self-sustaining.

St. Paul despises the culture of dependency, "If anyone is not willing to work, neither should that person eat" (2 Thessalonians 3:10).

The right to work is enshrined in the Universal Declaration of Human Rights; it is embedded also in the International Covenant on Economic, Social and Cultural Rights. Although unemployment is rampant in many countries of the world, no human being should accept to live in a state of redundancy.

Citizens everywhere have a duty and should have the courage to demand their rights to work. However, work should not become a mere ritual. As the English proverb goes, whatever is worth doing is also worth doing well - which means that all work must be done with considerable seriousness.

Hard work is a mark of courage while redundancy is a badge of cowardice and clumsiness. Lazy people tend to create excuses and always fear to face challenges. In so doing, they miss opportunities. "All life demands struggle…. The very striving and hard work that we so constantly try to avoid is the major building block in the person that we are today," said St John Paul VI.

Work is never devoid of challenges. Within it often arise difficulties in form of mistakes, accidents, sweat, tiredness, poor pay or even no pay. For the lazy person, the difficulties associated with work will become the justification for evading work, forgetting that all productive work requires an effort.

An Irish proverb says, "You must crack the nuts before you can eat the kernel."

A lazy person is consumed by odd thoughts and cannot take action until he is sure that no possible risk might arise from his decisions, "The lazy man says, 'There is a lion outside; it will kill me in the streets" (Proverbs 22:13).

A deep reflection, however, shows that risks are mere imaginations in a person's mind. The irony is that opportunities often come disguised as dangerous situations. People who bravely withstand the tensions of life, through hard work, usually reap great benefits. What one needs is to assess oneself positively and never to flee from duty.

Every human being - rich or poor, educated or illiterate, rural or urban, man or woman, youthful or aged - bears both the duty and opportunity to work and sustain their personal life other than relying on hand-outs from someone else. One of Africa's best minds ever, Julius Kambarage Nyerere, despises the culture of handouts. He promoted the concept of hard work. In his book, *Uhuru na Maendeleo4*[4] (1973) Nyerere writes, "A man is developing himself when he grows or earns enough to provide decent conditions for himself and his family; he is not being developed if someone gives him these things."

Scripture shows that God commissioned Jonah to preach to Nineveh so they could repent their wickedness. Jonah decided to evade the task; he took a voyage as he fled to Tarshish where he hoped there would be no more bother. Amidst the storms that almost drowned the entire ship, a fish swallowed Jonah. From inside the fish, prayed to God.

Thus he was rescued and empowered to accomplish the task assigned to him, "In my distress, I cried to Yahweh and he answered me" (Jonah 2:2-3).

---

4   Swahili for 'Freedom and Development'.

The fish belched him ashore before he proceeded to Nineveh and urged penitence. The king and all the people of Nineveh repented and fasted and God withdrew the impending punishment against that community. Jonah had underrated his own potential. He lacked confidence and self-esteem. He did not believe the king and his subjects could listen to him. Yet when he spoke, the results were instant and striking.

The task may be enormous but there is never a justification for evading responsibility. The right option is to seek God's guidance and protection to accomplish the task. God does not ignore the prayers of people who submit to Him.

Jesus Christ was at the verge of crucifixion but he still carried a heavy log on which he was to be hanged, "Carrying his own cross, he went out to the place of the Skull…" (John 19:17-18).

He was greatly troubled but he understood that however risky his mission appeared, it was manageable with God's will.

Jesus prayed earnestly, "My soul is full of sorrow, even to death…. Abba, Father, all things are possible for you; take this cup from me. Yet not what I want but what you want" (Mark 14:34-36).

In this episode, Jesus Christ demonstrated true human feelings. Fear is a natural human emotion which, nonetheless, should not lead a person to subdue his potential. Every person has a duty to overcome fear in order to register success.

Shakespeare says, "It is the part of men to fear and tremble."[5] On the other hand, Nelson Mandela (1918-2013) remarks, "I learned that courage was not the absence of fear, but the triumph over it."

Apply yourself fully to your work and present your fears to God in prayer. Daniel performed excellently and outshone all other administrators and governors. The king planned to give him authority over the entire kingdom because he was so trustworthy that neither corruption nor negligence could be found in him.

However, his peers teemed with envy and plotted against him. They persuaded the king to kill him for his commitment to God. As a result, he was thrown into a den of lions. His detractors hoped the beasts would devour him to death. Nevertheless, God sent an angel who closed the mouths of the lions and disabled them from harming him. Not even a single injury was inflicted on him because "he had trusted in God" (Daniel 6:3-23).

---

5   William Shakespeare (1599) in a play Julius Caesar, Act 1, Scene 3.

The story of Daniel proves that decency is a virtue to die for. God always minimises the possible risks that may arise from upright conduct. One should not violate ethics for momentary survival. Integrity demands that you stick to your work and uphold your noble beliefs even if public opinion does not favour you.

"Be strong and courageous, and do the work. Do not be afraid or discouraged, for the Lord God… will not fail you or forsake you until all the work … is finished (1 Chronicles 28:20).

Effective performance and ultimate success come from working very hard, with undivided attention and without seeking unfair advantage. The reason there is corruption in society is largely that many people want to earn salaries that are too disproportionate to their work. Some are happy to be paid for no work done while others find it easy to abandon work on flimsy excuses. In such circumstances, personal and national development will not occur.

Jesus Christ encourages dedicated work ethics, "No one who puts a hand to the plow and looks back is fit for the kingdom of God" (Luke 9:22).

Your family members are proud of you if you are hard working. Your neighbours and other community members will admire you if you are a diligent character. Your co-workers will respect you if you are a committed employee. Recruiters will be delighted to hire you if you are hardworking and trustworthy. Trivial matters like visiting friends or idle talk must not interrupt your work.

Prophet Nehemiah writes, "I am doing a great work and I cannot come down. Why should the work stop while I leave it and come down to you?" (Nehemiah 6:3).

Work is life. Hard work makes a man whole. As long as you are alive, you are required to labour and to labour hard. Time will come when you will be free from all work - and that time is after your death. A person who avoids work takes an early entry into the world of the dead!

"Fulfil your projects while you are able, for among the dead where you are going, there is no work, no planning, no knowledge, no wisdom" (Ecclesiastes 9:10).

RISE ABOVE MEAN CRITICISM

Aristotle says, "To avoid criticism say nothing, do nothing, be nothing."

My school life largely depended on what the school could offer. I was not the only one in this category but some students seemed to have everything they needed, including money for extra feeding. The school diet was at times so bad that someone had to get out buying what to eat such as sweet bananas and porridge. I could only manage this on rare occasions. In addition, having a girlfriend was considered smart.

Therefore, we always used weekend evenings to tell stories about our girlfriends. Most of the time, boys compiled holiday experiences for narrating to the peers during the school term. We would listen and interrogate each storyteller critically to determine if what he described was the truth.

The fact was that most of us were young and just beginning to be conscious of the attractiveness of the female person. However, it was embarrassing for anyone to plead guilty of failure to seduce a girl. Some boys did not have a relevant story to tell, so they would be mocked and despised. For fear of being laughed at, others made up stories of their love adventures. I belonged to the latter category.

One fateful evening, I was called upon to tell my story of the girl I had met during the holidays. I assured my listeners that I certainly had an amazing experience to share. Then I explained how I had engaged a beautiful lady in a love escapade. As I narrated, I saw some boys staring at each other, fighting to hold back their laughter. I began to lose my thread of thought. It became clear to all that I was just inventing the story and thus labouring to be coherent.

More trouble arose at question time. Someone asked which school my girl was attending and, before I could answer, everyone burst into laughter. Another demanded that I should show any love letter from the girlfriend. I did not have it.

It became clearer to me that they did not believe my story, all along. I became nervous. Someone else sought to know the name of my girlfriend but I had already perceived that I was getting embarrassed. Steven, a good friend of mine, was part the doubting group and I called out his name to divert attention and gain sympathy. This triggered louder and prolonged laughter.

"Steven?" several voices shouted as they laughed. "What a girlfriend!" they said.

I wished I could melt from their midst. I was branded as toothless, cowardly and mean. This was the last time that I participated in such a discussion.

People will always comment on something you do if it is worth their attention; and that is what is called 'criticism'. This word comes from the verb 'to criticise', which means to express dissatisfaction with someone or something. Because of its negative implications, criticism creates difficulties both for the critic and the one being criticised, especially based on their respective attitudes.

Humans naturally differ in preferences and opinions. Thus, some of their comments may be uncomfortable while others may be pleasant. If the intention of the criticiser is to despise, demoralise and humiliate the person criticised, it would be regarded as malicious, negative criticism.

Jesus Christ experienced this kind of criticism. The people of Galilee, his hometown, heard him preaching in their synagogue, questioned the authenticity of his message and treated him as an impostor.

They frowned at Him, "…… is this not the carpenter's son? Isn't his mother Mary…? Where then did he get all these things?' And they took offense at him…. " (Matthew 13:53-58).

In spite of the negative attitude of his tribesmen, Jesus performed some miracles in their town and then proceeded to people and places that would readily appreciate and embrace him.

To scorn Jesus on account of his known parentage bordered on prejudice. Social stereotypes generally use a person's known background to define his expected level of success. The standard behaviour is prescribed often based on such aspects as family, tribe, race, education, religion or gender.

Let no one despise you for your youth, but set the believers an example.

A person, who deviates from the socially constructed standards, though he may clearly be divinely inspired, will be greeted surely with criticism. If you are that person and are fainthearted, you will abandon the cause, devastated.

Norman Vincent Peale, author of *The Power of Positive Thinking* says, "The trouble with most of us is that we would rather be ruined by praise than saved by criticism."

This means that it becomes acceptable and essentially necessary to be criticised sometimes. When this happens, we should be in position to look out for the positive aspects of the criticism. In some cases, the criticiser seeks to point out genuine mistakes on the side of the person criticised in order to encourage improvement.

A person who lacks confidence and has low self-esteem, nevertheless, is most likely to be saddened, demoralised and infuriated by any form of criticism, even the tiniest dose. Such a person can easily become unkindly harsh to the criticiser and to other people. Only if you are an individual with a positive mental attitude would you be able to identify helpful features in a criticism where you are the target.

To find value in criticism, you must have two qualities: self- esteem and confidence. True, our society often exacts malicious criticisms but this should never be the reason for an individual to breakdown. For if you do, you miss the chance to benefit from constructive criticism, which is very necessary.

King Solomon again writes, "Poverty and disgrace come to him who ignores instruction, but whoever heeds reproof is honoured" (Proverbs 13: 18).

Similarly, German mathematics teacher, Johannes Kepler has said, "I much prefer the sharpest criticism of a single intelligent man to the thoughtless approval of the masses."

It is more dangerous when society applauds you for adhering to their wrong values, "Woe to you, when all people speak well of you, for so did their fathers to the false prophets" (Luke 6:26).

Innovative people tend to attract criticism since they are able to venture into areas where the community has limited exposure. They attempt to introduce light into areas that are known traditionally to be realms of darkness and, consequently, their actions invite criticisms from the masses. One must be ready to lead the way so that others can follow at their own time and pace. You have a duty to break the social bondages that might prevent you from realising your full potential, as Nelson Mandela and Barak Obama were able to. The two men rose above social limitations from ridiculed and seemingly ill-fated communities to become inspiring leaders of their respective nations.

Scripture counsels, "Let no one despise you for your youth, but set the believers an example in speech, in conduct, in love, in faith, in purity" (1 Timothy 4:12).

Although criticism is defined largely as a negative assessment of a person by another, its effect is particularly accentuated by the receiver's attitude. If you are willing to surrender to the condemnation of the critic, then his disapproval will have a negative effect on your wellbeing.

On the other hand, if you are not willing to absorb the malicious criticism, it will not have any effect on you. You must not break down and subdue your potential simply because of unfavourable public opinion.

As indicated above, submitting to the malicious, ill-informed standpoints of critics could easily obstruct a talented person from applying his skills or assuming responsibilities essential for his growth. The key to success is to know that what you are doing is right and, therefore, to exert sufficient energy to accomplish it.

Consequently, St Paul asserts that God will approve and bless your work: "If God is for us, who can be against us? (Romans 8:31)

LEARN TO INVEST

"I own quite a lot and I have worked very hard for it," once said Sudhir Ruparelia, a Ugandan entrepreneur who, in 2012, was ranked as the wealthiest individual in East Africa.

The miracle of success rarely ever falls from heaven like manna onto the individual who desires it. On the contrary, success arises from intentional obligation of resources and diligent application of effort as a form of investment. To invest is to dedicate your resources such as time, energy, money or effort to an activity or project in the expectation of a future benefit. It is a way of acquiring something that you can be able to use for a relatively long time.

A person who invests chooses to forego temporary satisfaction in order to enjoy greater achievement in the future. That person thinks beyond today's needs and understands that the present life of an individual, family or community essentially heralds a future state for which care and preparation are needful.

During my tenure as a student, Muntuyera High School and Ruyonza School were going to play a friendly football match. Ruyonza School was found about seventy kilometres away in Bushenyi District. Our school was gripped with anxiety as the process of selecting the students to accompany the football team started.

The criterion was clear. Priority was given to active footballers, prefects, team members of other games, known cheerleaders and students who were known to be supportive during sports events. I wanted to attend the contest at Ruyonza School but I lacked all the requirements. I checked with my best friend, Devance, to discover that he faced the same dilemma. We were a boring lot and our classmates referred to us as mere bookworms.

We tried to persuade the teacher in charge to add our names to the list but he said there was no more space on the school lorry. Yet, we did not want to miss this trip. Unfortunately, we could not privately raise money for the fares in the public transport arena. Devance came up with a crazy proposal: we should walk to Ruyonza School.

"We have our feet," he argued. "Why should we beg for free transport? Why should we miss the trip?" he emphasised.

It was not a bad idea but it meant we had to cover the whole distance without taking a drink or food. The next morning, we left the school very early in the morning and missed breakfast because the journey was long. We walked at a speed of six kilometres per hour and covered about thirty kilometres by around eleven o'clock. We had started the journey trotting vigorously but we grew slower the further we went. We became tired and hungry midway. We faced a crisis. It became clear that we could not make it to the venue of the match in time, thus we contemplated returning to our school. We sat in a tree shade by the roadside as we mulled over our situation.

It was then that we heard a group of youths, singing from a distance. Listening carefully, we noticed that it was the team from our school aboard the lorry. The lucky students were singing and shouting joyfully while we weathered the wrath of the sun and hunger. We also feared the teacher would recognise us on the road and have us dismissed from school or given heavy punishment for taking such a silly move.

Initially, we agreed to hide in the nearby bush to allow the group pass without noticing us. On second thought, Devance proposed that we could wait by the road and jump into the truck as it moved past. I had never done this in my life so I objected. Before we could resolve the matter, the lorry approached. Devance grasped the bar by the hind entrance. The students recognised him and, grabbing his hand, pulled him inside.

I remained on the ground alone but the students urged me to follow suit. I was too tired and worried to run successfully after a moving truck. At the same time, I had already lost company and would either stay down and suffer immensely alone or take the risk and join other students on the vehicle.

I had about five seconds to make a decision. As I summoned my feet to carry me forward, I closed my eyes, raised my hands and shot towards the lorry. I felt floating in the air as someone held me by hand. I opened my eyes for a moment to find students hugging me excitedly inside the lorry.

At Ruyonza School, we had lunch with other students, before we attended the match later in the day. Finally, we returned to our school and our colleagues received us triumphantly. Devance and I had invested our feet, sweat and effort to attend the football match. Scripture offers countless situations of investment but, in this essay, we shall focus on five elements namely: foresight, strategic planning, innovation, self-denial, and sacrifice.

Foresight is the ability to think ahead; a person's capacity to look far into the distant void and see the concealed treasure. We can term as foresight, Abram's behaviour, when he was called.

Abram got a clear idea of God's promise to make him "a great nation… a blessing … (and) went as Yahweh had told him…" (Genesis 12:2-4).

Although he was already aged seventy-five, he could still dream of a better future. Accordingly, he has been ranked as the grandfather of all believers. He sacrificed the favourable company of his family and local community and ventured into the unknown in obedience to God.

This was a high cost for an on old man to pay but, as the Russians proverbially say, "To know that candles are very expensive is of no value only to the blind."

The parable of the ten brides also presents another case of foresight. The hopeful girls expected the groom to arrive early but he delayed until very late in the night. However, five of the ten brides had kept some fuel in reserve for fear of being plunged into darkness should the waiting time be longer. On the other hand, five of the brides only carried fuel to last for the estimated short waiting time. They did not expect the groom to delay and, when he did, they run out of fuel. They should have invested in fuel early enough because money could not be a useful substitute in the circumstances. Yes, they had the money to buy more fuel but as the popular proverb teaches, "Time is of more value than money because it is possible to get more money than someone but you cannot get more time."

The five foolish brides may represent people who never think ahead and thus fail to plan for the future; directing all their efforts to today's needs and thus failing to save for 'the rainy day'. As they went out looking for more fuel, the groom arrived. The five brides who had carried extra fuel received him.

The wise brides enjoyed the much awaited wedding exclusively since they had planned properly (Matthew 25:4-10). They understood the value of money and, ultimately, used it in time for its rightful purpose.

Socrates who is credited as one of the founders of Western philosophy says, "…virtue does not come from money, but from virtue comes money and all other good things to man… and to the state."

Warren Edward Buffet, regarded as the most successful investor of the twentieth century says, "It's nice to have a lot of money but you know, you don't want to keep it around forever…. Otherwise, it's a little like saving sex for your old age."

Strategic planning is another ingredient of investment. This is the drawing of a sketch design of a perfect, finished project. A good plan guides and motivates an individual and his supporters to perform tasks with zeal. Such a plan should therefore be attractive from the start to inspire the owner and to give a good first impression to the public.

The Scripture points out, "Everyone serves the best wine first, and then when people have drunk enough, he serves that which is ordinary" (John 2:10).

Jesus Christ poses a crucial question about strategic planning, "Do you build a house without first sitting down to count the cost and see if you have enough to complete it? (Luke 14:28)

Meaningful investment demands careful planning as Buffet again says, "What a wise man does in the beginning, the fool does in the end."

Investment also demands innovation. Nothing drives home the concept of innovation more than the parable of the talents. A king entrusted a pound to each of his servants. When he checked later, one servant had invested and multiplied the pound ten times. Another servant had multiplied the pound five times. Both were rewarded with power and wealth.

The king, however, found a servant who had maintained the pound at its base value. This servant argued that he understood the king to be a strict superintendent whose money had to be handled with great care. That servant was roundly condemned for being too idle to improve the value of the pound (Luke 19:11-25).

People like this indolent servant need counsel from Isabel Dos Santos who was named Angola's first billionaire and the richest woman in Africa as of March 2013 - she once said, "I think there are a lot of people with family connections but who are actually nowhere. If you are hardworking and determined, you will make it and that's the bottom line. I don't believe in an easy way through." The initial pound God has given everyone is life, complete with all intellectual faculties and body organs. You breathe free air like any other person; you have the same number of hours in a day as all other people. There are many other God-given resources at your disposal, including soil, light, plants and water. As a person, your potential to achieve success is so abundant; you only need to detect and utilise all the opportunities available to you.

God said, "I have given you every seed-bearing plant… every tree that bears fruit…" (Genesis 1:29).

In addition, success demands self-denial as a form of investment. This means setting aside your cherished needs, wishes, and interests for a cause. Self-denial means that even though you may be certain of your advantages and pleasures, you make a choice to set them aside for a greater good. The higher the price you are willing to pay, the greater the dividends you might earn.

Innovators such as inventors are willing to give up comfort for the greater good

Thomas Paine,[6] a political activist and philosopher who authored two influential pamphlets at the start of the American Revolution and ultimately inspired the rebels to declare independence from Britain says, "What we obtain too cheap, we esteem too lightly; it is dearness only that gives everything its value."

---

6   Thomas Paine was born in Great Britain in 1737 and died in New York in 1809.

Jesus Christ also counsels, "Deny yourself, take up your cross…" (Mark 8:34).

To register success, you must be ready to take risks, which requires that you take a leap into unfamiliar situations that you have no experience about and are unsure of the exact consequences therefrom. Many successful people in history have left their comfort zones and ventured into unusual situations whereby their choices might be viewed as weird for taking risks and actions which other people could not think of.

All the inventors, explorers, missionaries, investors, revolutionaries, and other famous people have become leaders in their various fields by taking risks with their lives. They would opt for self-denial instead even though there would be opportunities for them to swim in luxury. All responsibility is leadership, and people normally gather around selfless characters.

"The good shepherd gives up his life for his sheep (John 10:11). The closest companion of investment is, perhaps, sacrifice.

One of Africa's most illustrious sons, Stephen Saad, has said, "In life, you don't get anywhere or do anything you hope to without some sort of sacrifice." Saad was a famous investor. He was a co- founder of Aspen Pharmacare, a highly rated drug manufacturer in South Africa. Investment and sacrifice almost always go hand- in-hand.

Scripture shows that it was not an easy decision that Abraham would abandon the country and family of his birth for the Promised Land. He knew nothing about his new area of settlement. He accepted, nonetheless, to venture into the unknown and earned his fame.

During their liberation, the Israelites faced such starvation that they almost perished in the wilderness (Exodus 17:3). The apostles of Jesus too left their properties and families to become missionaries, having got revelations of the eventual heavenly glory. Jesus Christ assured them, "… no one who has left a house or brothers or sisters or father or mother or children or lands… who will not receive his reward… he will receive a hundred times… (Mark 10:29-30).

All the martyrs and saints in Christian history were people who gave up major worldly glories, including their lives, to attain higher virtues. To register success, therefore, you must make sacrifices.

Jesus Christ proclaims, "Unless the grain… dies, it remains alone; but if it dies, it produces much fruit" (John 12:24).

BECOME A POSITIVE THINKER

"Consider yourselves fortunate, my brothers and sisters, when you meet with every kind of trial, for you know that the testing of your faith makes you steadfast" (James 1:2-3).

Every opportunity presents with obstacles, while every obstacle presents some opportunities. The ability to see opportunities in an obstacle lies in a person's attitude. It is only a person who is a positive thinker that is able to see the opportunity in every difficulty.

In his *Lady Windermere's Fan*, Oscar Wilde (1995) says, "We are all in the gutter but some of us are looking at the stars."

I joined Muntuyera High School without many of the basic necessities. In fact, I did not have shoes. Sebo gave me his own pair, which was several inches too big for an adolescent that I was. Thus I did not wear shoes for the first two years in the school. I kept the pair clean in my metallic box, always ready to pull them out in case a teacher demanded to see if I had shoes.

Later in my fourth year, I was required, like all my peers, to raise additional money to take part in an academic trip to the Rwenzori region. It was going to be an expensive but memorable expedition. I knew too well that it was impossible to get the money from my parents but I was determined to participate in the trip. I decided to join the gangs smuggling coffee out of the country to the neighbouring Republic of Rwanda where prices were very high. Like all profitable ventures, coffee smuggling was largely unsafe. Smugglers walked on foot, at night and without rest until they crossed the national border. They would not use the conventional pathways. The activity was illegal. Armed militias, who could easily shoot dead any suspected lawbreaker, patrolled the highways. The footpath was infested with thorny shrubs, so every participant was certain to suffer injuries, not to mention the fierce beasts like hyenas, leopards and hippos that often attacked the caravans.

The trekkers also had to cross deep, fast flowing water bodies in the areas of Rwempasha and Nyabweshongoize. In many cases, robbers also appeared disguised as law enforcers and would force the smugglers to discard the loads of coffee and disperse back home. With all these risks in mind, therefore, the smugglers would each carry a spear or other defensive object and often confronted the attackers. In one such skirmish, a village chief known as Benura, who was participating in the smuggling, was speared to death.

Other than missing the school academic trip, I was determined to face these challenges. At the beginning of the school vacation, I reached home ready to proceed to join the smuggling campaign but I was too late. The gang had left a day earlier!

I thought of another option to raise money. Nyabo had saved a little money from the sale of a dozen pineapples from my garden. With it, I would buy some bananas and brew local alcohol, *tonto*, which I would sell and earn. The bananas were ripe in five days so I woke up one morning to squeeze them to generate juice. A stronger adult would have done a better job, so the bananas went bad and I was unable to produce juice. I should have hired a mature man to do the job since it only required payment of about five litres of the liquor. What an unfortunate mistake!

My hope to travel with classmates for the academic trip was dashed. I had even lost my little income from the pineapples. At the beginning of the school term, Sebo only gave me a half of the school dues and I returned to school. I tried very much to avoid groups that were discussing how interesting the trip was likely to be. This was the boys' obsession every night at bedtime.

A teacher, named Johnnie, found out that my name was missing from the list of the students scheduled for the trip. When he asked me, I told him I was not going to participate since I did not have the money. He sympathised and empathised. He offered money, to my excitement. I was going to realise my dream of, possibly, becoming the first person from my village to make such a trip.

Scripture shows that David was very young, armed with only stones and a sling, when he confronted Goliath in the battlefield. On the other hand, Goliath "…was about three metres tall. He wore a helmet of bronze and a coat covered with bronze scales. His armour weighed sixty kilograms. He had bronze gloves strapped on his legs and a bronze spear slung between his shoulders. The shaft of his spear was the size of a weaver's rod; its head weighed seven kilos. His shield-bearer went before him. When he uttered threats, the entire rival armed forces trembled.

However, "David said to Saul, 'Let no one be discouraged by this Philistine…. Saul told David, 'You cannot fight with this Philistine for you are still young…. David… picked up five smooth stones… rushed to the battleground and struck the Philistine on the forehead… and he fell on his face to the ground…. David triumphed…" (1 Samuel 17: 4-58).

As the proverb goes, "What matters is not the size of the dog in the fight, but the size of the fight in the dog."

Again, it is said in Nigeria, "When a man says 'yes', his *chi* also says 'yes.'" It is believed that each man has a personal god known as *'chi'*.

With a positive mind-set, every situation can be overcome. Victory is largely derived from a person's state of mind. The Bible shows that all you need to succeed, in all your endeavours, is unshakable faith, or what is known as a positive attitude.

In the course of the exodus, the Israelites literally came to the end of the road as they stumbled upon the Red Sea, along their escape route. This posed a very serious danger since the Egyptians trailed them with chariots and warriors.

The Israelites would have perished at one point in their trek. Either their chasers would have slaughtered them or they would have drowned into the sea. The situation was so dire that they saw no chance of possible survival. In the midst of this dilemma, however, the most unlikely thing happened! "Moses stretched out his hand over the sea and Yahweh made a strong east wind blow…. The waters divided and the sons of Israel walked on dry ground through the middle of the sea, with the waters forming a wall on their right and to their left" (Exodus 14:21-22).

At another point, the Israelites experienced terrible shortage of water for both themselves and their animals. They were in the desert where lack of water is a natural condition. They were in such a state of hopelessness that they believed Moses had blundered by bringing them out of the Egypt, where they were slaves, to such an isolated, barren place.

Yet Moses did not lose his faith and, when all the others were in despair, God provided water in a miraculous manner. If there was any place they would have looked out to draw water from, it would certainly never have been a stone.

However, "Moses raised his hand and struck the rock… then water in abundance gushed out for the community and their livestock to drink" (Numbers 20:11).

Faith led Moses to invite people to gather around a rock for water as though it was a stream

The Scripture also presents the story of Peter walking on water. He was only an ordinary person like any other apostle. Yet he was not afraid to take a daring step.

When Jesus appeared to the apostles, majestically walking on water, they were all "…terrified, thinking it was a ghost" (Matthew 14:26).

In contrast, Peter was not completely alarmed. He was the only one who gathered confidence and sought the grace to walk on water too. Indeed, he was able to get out of the boat and walked some distance on the water. He managed to do so as long as he had the faith and courage to go on. It is only when he lost confidence that he started sinking.

St Matthew writes, "Peter got out of the boat and walked on the water to go to Jesus. But seeing the strong wind, he was afraid and began to sink…" (Matthew 14:29-30).

The Gospel of St Mark presents a story of an official of the synagogue, named Jairus, who displayed amazing faith when his daughter was on the verge of death. Jairus sought Jesus' intervention but as the Lord headed to the place where the sick girl was, information came that she was already dead. Jesus got the news but ignored the pessimistic messengers.

Some people told Jairus, "Your daughter is dead. Why trouble the Master any further…" (Mark 5:35).

Jesus said to Jairus, "'Do not fear. Just believe?'…. Jesus entered the home of the official and said to the mourners, 'The child is not dead but asleep'. They laughed at him…. The girl got up at once and began to walk around" (Mark 5:36-42).

From this incident, it is clear that the girl's father went to Jesus with firm faith that he could provide a solution to the situation that was evidently out of hand. Even when he was told that the girl was already dead, he was not shuttered since Jesus had accepted to intervene. Jesus restored the girl's life, and this served to strengthen the man's faith even more.

The Nigerians say, "In the moment of crisis, the wise build bridges while the foolish build dams."

After a bout of illness, Lazarus of Bethany died and was buried.

Many people from the neighbourhood turned up to condole with the bereaved family of Martha and Mary. Jesus had missed seeing Lazarus during his sickness and only arrived at their home when Lazarus had been in the tomb for four days. The natural belief was that his body was already putrid.

When Jesus demanded that the tomb should be reopened, Martha protested, "Lord, by now he will smell, for this is the fourth day" (v.39).

Jesus, nonetheless, "…cried out in a loud voice, 'Lazarus, come out!' The dead man came out…" (John 11:1-44).

The event of the resurrection of Lazarus means that there is no situation, however desperate, that God cannot stabilise.

In another episode, a miserable widow lived in the town of Naim and was extremely unfortunate to lose his only son. The only help her community members could give was to gather at her home and offer a hand in burying the young man. Fortunately, Jesus came across the mourners as they took the dead body to the burial site. No one had any imagination that the situation could be reversed at such a point. The widow was very sorrowful indeed.

"When the Lord saw her, he had pity on her… he came up and touched the stretcher… then said, 'Young man, I say to you, wake up'. And the dead man sat up and began to speak, and Jesus gave him to his mother" (Luke 7:11-15).

There is another amazing story of Peter's miraculous escape from prison. King Herod killed two brotherly apostles: James and John. He also arrested and imprisoned Peter, with tacit intentions to kill him too. He ensured that Peter was firmly chained and guarded. He had no chance to escape. However, God would not allow Herod's plans to materialise.

"Peter was sleeping between two soldiers, bound by a double chain, while guards kept watch at the gate of the prison…. The angel… woke him up…. At once, the chains fell from Peter's wrists…. They passed the first guard, then the second… and the iron door leading out to the city, which opened of itself…. They went out…" (Acts 12:1-10).

There was no need for anxiety on the part of Peter. Once he acknowledged the possibility of freedom, the prison doors opened by themselves.

After Jesus' crucifixion, the Pharisees and chief priests wanted to ensure that he would not get out of the tomb by any means.

"So they went to the tomb … sealed the stone and secured it" (Matthew 27:66). However, "…an angel of the Lord descending from heaven came to the stone, rolled it from the entrance of the tomb…. The guards trembled in fear…" (Matthew 28:2-4).

All this happened according to Jesus' earlier prophecy, "The Son of Man will be delivered into the hands of men. They will kill him, but three days after he has been killed, he will rise (Mark 9:31). In any difficult situation, there is always a potential solution.

Primarily, the crisis is often born in the individual's mind and is manifested physically on the outside. It is your perception of the situation at hand that defines your ultimate status.

The sixteenth President of the United States of America, who is credited for abolishing slavery in the country, Abraham Lincoln counsels thus: "We can complain because rose bushes have thorns, or rejoice because thorn bushes have roses".

Similarly, Wayne W. Dyer says, "With everything that has happened to you, you either feel sorry for yourself or treat what has happened as a gift. Everything is either an opportunity to grow or an obstacle to keep you from growing."

Once you have worked on your mentality, the inevitable happens as Don Moen sings in his hymnal lyrics, "God will make a way, where there seems to be no way …"

HAVE A PURPOSE IN LIFE

*The mystery of human existence lies not in just staying alive, but in finding something to live for - **Fyodor Dostoyevsky.***

The teacher is the most important person one could become. I got this impression during my primary school days. Our teachers spoke English with ease. While everyone in the community woke up every morning, wore tatters and headed to gardens to till the soil, teachers dressed up smartly and went to school to teach.

Only the priest seemed to be superior to the teacher. Whenever he visited the school, the teachers left the front bench for him, joined us in the audience and followed all his instructions. They would clap hands, sing, kneel and stand up as the priest demanded. He would even tell them how they should treat the learners.

None of us, however, could dream of becoming a priest because we believed that such a job was reserved for foreigners, especially white men. It would be too hard for one to understand the secrets of God the way the priest did. As he preached, he talked about God with such sureness that it was clear the two interacted very closely. It was amazing how he would explain clearly what God wanted people do.

I wanted to become a teacher from the beginning. I admired teachers because they wielded enormous authority intellectually and socially. As children, we saw that our parents exercised a lot of power at home but they always became humble whenever they encountered teachers. A teacher could compel a parent to come to the school on a definite day and time.

In addition, a teacher could introduce a concept none of us had ever heard of and explain it effectively for us to understand. He could draw a map of any part of the world and plot locations of specific geographical features. He could read any book, understand and simplify the content for us. Most of the primary school teachers could teach any subject in any class.

Teachers also instructed us about the acceptable dress code at school and at home. A teacher could penalise a child even outside the school. They taught us about personal and family hygiene. They told us about how to relate among ourselves as learners and how to relate with our parents and other elders.

If a teacher gave an academic task, he could leisurely mark any answer wrong even if a learner believed that he had correctly answered a question. I cannot forget the day we studied about carnivores - animals that eat meat. The teacher wrote names of animals on the chalkboard and asked us to identify which ones could eat meat. Some of the animals included: lion, cow, goat, dog, sheep and cat.

We believed that only human beings, not animals, could eat meat. To guide us, the teacher said that one animal which ate meat as its primary diet was a dog. The whole class burst into laughter. We thought he was just trying to be funny or it was a slip of the tongue. To make life easy for us, he added that the other animals that ate meat were cats and lions. Again, we laughed in disapproval. The teacher was shocked and asked why we appeared doubtful.

"A dog eats bones," several pupils shouted out. "A cat eats rats," others said. "A lion eats people," we told him.

The teacher laughed too. Then, he explained that when a cat eats a rat, it is actually eating the meat in the rat - and so does a dog when it grabs a bone and a lion when it eats a person. We saw no logic in his explanation. None of us agreed because we knew that meat is obtained from a butchery for human consumption and we had never seen a rat or a person slaughtered for meat. In our villages, we also saw that dogs only fed on bones thrown to them after people had eaten all the meat.

One teacher, Paul, was particularly very inspiring to me. He spoke English most of the time, wore glasses whenever he wanted to read a book, wrote in neat letters on the chalkboard, had a glittering bicycle and cracked jokes during his lessons. I just wanted to become such a teacher. In secondary school, the teachers were even more impressive.

After attaining the advanced certificate of education, I wanted to join the department of education for my tertiary studies to become a professional teacher. When I indicated it as my first choice, however, the Director of Studies summoned me to his office and persuaded me to change the course.

He advised me, "You can become a lawyer, a journalist or a social scientist - not a teacher."

I amended my choices to make education the last of my preferred options. When the results were made public, however, I had obtained such humble scores that I could only get admitted for education studies. My childhood dream to become a teacher was fulfilled. A teacher I became, finally!

A Ghanaian proverb says, "Nature gave us two cheeks instead of one to make it easier to eat hot food."

Indeed, everything that exists does for a purpose. So is every human being.

The book of Jeremiah proclaims, "Even before I formed you in the womb, I have known you. Even before you were born, I had set you apart..." (Jeremiah 1:4-5).

To be 'set apart' means that you, as a person, are endowed with a distinct character, talents and abilities. There is no other person with exactly your attributes: physical appearance, parentage, place of origin, time of birth, beliefs and everything you are, which all constitute your personality. As a unique being, therefore, God created you for a purpose. You are not an idle organism brought to life by accidental occurrence.

You are not an object fashioned by dint of a purposeless system. God knew you before you were conceived in your mother's womb. He sanctioned your birth and continues to sustain your life for good reasons. It is important to think seriously about God's purpose for you and to work hard to meet His expectations.

"You were put on this earth to achieve your greatest self, to live out your purpose, and to do it courageously," says Steve Maraboli (2009) in *Life, the Truth, and Being Free.*

When you are aware of the purpose of your being, God will be at hand to see you through any challenges that may arise as you pursue success in your life. You will confidently go about your work, since working hard proves that you are conscious of the purpose for which you were created.

This shows that you have a vision for your life because: "Where there is no vision, people get out of hand..." (Proverbs 29:18).

A vision is the mental idea of the state of life you want to attain and the footprint you want to leave on the world.

In the novel, *The Brothers Karamazov*, Fyodor Dostoyevsky (1980) states, "The mystery of human existence lies not in just staying alive, but in finding something to live for."

Jesus Christ faced enormous challenges on earth but still lived a purposeful life. He did not submit to the suppressive pressures he encountered, because he understood his personal relevance on earth.

During his encounter with Pilate shortly before the crucifixion, Jesus said, "For that purpose, I was born and for this purpose, I have come to the world" (John 18:37).

You must know your purpose in life and work very hard to reach your dreams. By working hard, you earn God's favour. He will bless your efforts and you will enjoy a rewarding life. As a branch yields fruits to fulfil the purpose of a tree, you too must do productive work to make God's purpose a reality in your life.

Scripture says, "God prunes every vine branch that bears fruit so that it may bear even more fruits" (John 15:2).

In modern times, however, humanity has experienced the sad reality of unemployment, especially in the developing world. Young people's dreams of 'good' jobs are largely shattered by the shrinking availability of jobs, limited skills as well as a borderless world order that has produced a free labour market and thus easily subjects the local citizenry to stiff competition with more experienced, better trained, or well financed players from other countries. As a result, many people remain 'unemployed' or 'underemployed'.

Not 'What did he get'? But 'What did he do'?

Unemployment should neither promote nor justify idleness. It is incumbent on someone to look out for opportunities in areas where others may not imagine success could be derived. The type of job one ends up doing does not determine the level of success or fulfilment one would experience.

One wonders why corruption thrives in what are generally considered as 'decent' jobs; while most honest workers are people doing 'humble' jobs. Corruption might be evidence that the worker does not feel fulfilled, in spite of being advantaged with a gainful job. This means one does not have to give up on life simply because they did not get a lucrative job.

A person who is likely to find fulfilment in a highly rewarding job is also likely to derive joy from handling a modest job because happiness is only an attitude. It is borne of one's desire to be useful to self and society - to have a purpose.

When the voice of God called out, "Whom shall I send?" Isaiah did not hesitate to answer, "Here I am. Send me!" (Isaiah 6:8).

By the time he asked to be sent, Isaiah was fully aware of the purpose he would serve and he did not disappoint. He is possibly the greatest prophet of the Old Testament. Yet, in embracing the mission, Isaiah was inspired by neither the fame nor the comfort he was likely to experience in doing the job. He embraced God's purpose.

It is therefore a core responsibility that you should seriously reflect on your goals in life by which you would be able to realise God's purpose for you. Do you have a job? Are you in school? Do you have a family? Whoever you are, you must do your work with steadfast commitment. The worth of a man is determined by the quality of the work they do. One must not give excuses for any dismal performance of their tasks.

Incidentally, many people who hold responsibilities are initially anxious to get the jobs but once they are employed, their commitment wanes day-by-day. It is one thing to get a job but it is another thing to do the job well. Anything that is worth doing is also worth doing very well. Work is always an opportunity for you to prove your worth and purpose.

In the poem, *"The Measure of a Man"*, St. Longinus states:

Not - How did he die? But - How did he live? Not - What did he gain? But - What did he give? These are the things that measure the worth Of a man as a man, regardless of birth.

Not - What was his station? But – had he a heart? And - How did he play his God-given part?

The Bible also gives a story of a poor widow who dropped her only coin into the offering box when time for making financial contributions came. Although her participation in the offertory demanded that she should surrender her very last coin, she did not look for an excuse to exempt her from tithing.

Seeing the widow's munificence, Jesus Christ praised her. "Truly I say to you, this poor widow put in more than all those who gave offerings… she gave from her poverty, and put in everything she had, her very living" (Mark 11:41-44).

As St John Paul II said, "No one is so poor that he has nothing to give." In the eyes of other people, the poor widow's coin was disgraceful. Yet, she dropped it into the temple treasury with unusual confidence. She attached value and a sense of purpose to her act. Ultimately, she earned accolades from the Lord. Her offering is a direct indictment on the men and women who suppress their talents and resources based on f limsy excuses.

In the same way, the simple job or business you do should not bring regrets and misery in your life. Rather, it should infect you with joy for it is your attitude that would give value to what you do. People may give excuses like these: "I will not work hard because my job is junior, my salary is small"; "I cannot help because I am poor, I do not own a car"; "I cannot participate because I am young"; "I cannot compete because I am not highly educated".

In your status, there is a purpose you must serve and serve it with enthusiasm. Do your best to contribute to the welfare of society. You may not have money or other physical resources to give out. Yet you can contribute ideas during meetings, workshops and seminars. You can write a letter to a newspaper editor for publication about human welfare. You can participate in street cleaning activities. You can become a member of a church choir.

Excellence comes more from personal commitment and self- assurance than from competence. What you need is to recognise your purpose, unlock your potential and pursue success regardless of life's countless challenges.

TRY TO GO AN EXTRA MILE

"The value of a sheep is in its tail," an African proverb teaches.

The sheep's tail looks as a minor element. You can be tempted to dismiss it as an irrelevant aspect to a sheep because it is located behind and does not seem to play an active role in the sheep's life. Some people even cut part of it off to enable the sheep grow healthier.

What we know is that the sheep is a fatty animal. Its fame originates from its tail. The tail is the store for most of a sheep's fats. The lesson is that it is not enough to make maximum use of our basic talents. One should also look beyond one's obvious strengths and deploy their minor skills to register success. This is known as 'going an extra mile'.

After school, I started teaching. I was anxious to be the good teacher that I had dreamt of becoming since childhood. I understood that the students looked to me for direction in the fields of academics, discipline, life skills and general decorum.

Whereas I believed I had so much to offer, I was retained as a mere teacher of English for a whole year. I wanted to become a class teacher, a club patron, a director of studies, a member of the school board, a head of department, a school editor or a minutes' secretary. None of these came to me, being a new teacher. Such roles were reserved for the 'senior teachers' who were considered mature and experienced.

Not all 'senior teachers', however, had other assignments beyond the specific teaching subjects. Some of them were not different from new teachers. There was a risk, therefore, that I could remain an ordinary subject teacher for a long part of my career. So I would not progress to become a head teacher or a district education officer.

I decided that I should not wait for the head teacher to assign me additional responsibilities. I knew only too well that I could do more than I was doing. I felt I was underemployed and hence needed effective deployment. I developed a concept and submitted it to the head teacher for approval to create the Aids Concern Club in the school. This approach was not conventional. The school management systems such as the Ministry of Education and Board of Governors primarily initiated and endorsed all the students' clubs. The method I used revealed me as a deviant character, so my proposal was initially vetoed. I was asked to provide serious proof that the new club would not be a duplication of the existing ones.

As I laboured to articulate the need for a new club, it dawned on me that it would not address any serious gaps. In the end, I mentioned to the head teacher that I needed a platform to engage with the students and make a greater contribution to their growth. On that note, she allowed me to form the club.

When I announced the creation of the Aids Concern Club and introduced its objectives to the students, the response was overwhelming. It became, possibly, the most popular club in the school within a year. Soon, I was appointed as a member of the school editorial board, a nutrition advisor and a class teacher. I began to view myself as a future head teacher.

This was before I left teaching to work for a nongovernmental organisation. It was an uphill task as I did not know how to use a computer, which was the principal equipment by which all work was done. I had previously been handwriting all my work in school. Therefore, I needed to go an extra mile if I was to fit in the scope of nongovernmental organisations.

I gave up my weekends and used them to learn working with a computer. I volunteered to draft and edit other people's activity reports. This gave me an opportunity to enhance my computer skills. Indirectly, I had appointed myself as a reviewer of many team members' reports. In a couple of years, I was posted to neighbouring countries, Tanzania and Malawi, to provide technical assistance to the respective teams in development work.

People who go an extra mile in their work are those who are willing to perform their tasks beyond expectations. During job performance appraisals, workers who achieve beyond expectations often earn job promotions, impressive salary increments, performance awards or other forms of recognition.

Jesus Christ taught that it is important to exceed targets when we are doing our work, "If someone strikes you on the right cheek, turn to him the left one also.... If someone forces you to go one mile, go with him two miles" (Matthew 5:39-41).

People who go an extra mile are willing to perform their tasks beyond expectations.

Some people might assume that Jesus encourages people to be submissive. This is not the case. He actually teaches that a person should never be satisfied by doing only what is basic. We have the capacity to achieve much more than we can imagine, if we do not maintain things at their face value.

The Bible presents a relevant scenario in the parable of the talents. Three servants were entrusted with special resources. "The man who had received the five talents went at once and put his money to work and gained five more. So also the one with the two talents gained two more" (Matthew 25: 16-17).

To go an extra mile requires creativity which these two servants clearly exhibited and were rewarded for. The third servant, who retained the talent in its original state, was not merely despised but his talent was taken away and given to those who could multiply it. The disciples on the road to Emmaus met a lone traveller and tried to protect him from danger. They told him about the brutal crucifixion of Jesus. They did not stop at warning him about the unsafe environment prevailing in that area but they also compelled him to stay with them and resume the journey at daybreak.

"But they strongly urged him, 'Stay with us for it is almost evening; the day is nearly over" (Luke 24:28-29).

By describing the recent brutal events to him, one can say that they had already given him enough information. Yet they went an extra mile as they became too concerned about his safety and insisted that he should not proceed on his journey alone. As a result of their extra care, they discovered that it was not a stranger but the resurrected Lord, Jesus.

In the parable of the Good Samaritan, there is a sympathetic traveller who would have done one or two things for the injured man and left. He was not from his tribe. He was not socially required to provide help to the injured man. He did not know him. However, he did more and more to save his life. Although he was a stranger, the Good Samaritan would not think that he had done enough until the man was cured completely.

"He bandaged his wounds, pouring on oil and wine… he put the man on his own donkey, brought him to an inn and took care of him… he took out two silver coins and gave them to the innkeeper. 'Look after him,' he said, 'and when I return I will reimburse you for any extra expense you may have" (Luke 10:34-35).

Another case is of the ten lepers Jesus Christ once healed. All they desired was healing and they got it. Thereafter, nine of the lepers imagined that they had no more business with Jesus and went their different ways. Only one felt that it was not enough to experience the joy of good health; he also needed to express gratitude to the Lord.

"One of them, when he saw he was healed, came back praising God in a loud voice. He threw himself at the feet of Jesus and thanked him…" (Luke 17:15-16).

It was indeed such a simple duty that the majority failed to perform. This possibly explains why so many people become failures in life because they miss out on simple acts. Once they realise what they consider as their bigger targets, they forget about the minor details which are necessary to make the accomplishment wholesome.

One time, the apostles had spent the night fishing. They did not catch fish and emerged from the activity very tired. In a way, they had wasted their time and effort and, therefore, ought to have been very frustrated to return from the lake empty-handed.

In every job, one needs to put in extra effort in order to shine. As experienced fishermen, they understood that night-time was the ideal period to catch fish, not during daytime. They should have spent the day resting in preparation for another attempt in the next night. When Jesus advised them to cast the nets into the lake in broad daylight, they did not claim that the fishing time was over. They were willing to put in extra effort and time.

"When they did, they were unable to haul the nets because of the big number of fish they caught" (John 21:3-6).

Martin Luther King Jr says, "If a man is called to be a street sweeper, he should sweep streets so well that all the hosts of heaven and earth will pause to say, 'Here lived a great street sweeper who did his job well.'"

The Scripture also reveals that when the apostles learnt that Jesus had resurrected, "Peter and the other disciple went running, but the other disciple outran Peter and ... looked in at the strips of linen lying there .... Then Simon Peter came along behind him and went straight into the tomb. Finally the other disciple, who had reached the tomb first, also went inside" (John 20:3-8).

In the circumstances, running was very ideal as part of the whole event. What was required was not merely the speed to get to the tomb first, neither was it to stand within its vicinity, but to get inside it and confirm that the Lord was risen indeed. We always must take the final step to register success - by going an extra mile.

BECOME A FLEXIBLE PERSON

Flexibility is the 'ability to bend without breaking'.

The Japanese have a proverb, "The bamboo that bends is stronger than the oak that resists."

The oak tree is an important component of hardwood forests and is ranked among the world's strongest woods. On the other hand, the bamboo belongs to the grass family, has a hollow stem and is generally a soft plant.

In hard times, however, it is a tree with a flexible stem that is able to withstand a storm. The one with a hard stem breaks in the face of a strong wind. This is echoed in an African proverb, "You must be willing to bend if you do not want to break."

When a person is flexible, he is able to adapt to new situations including unfamiliar events that arise in the course of life. Flexibility enables a person to receive and utilise new ideas from various sources such as conversations, publications, mass media, get-togethers or even private meditations.

Adherence to God's word often thrives on the softness of character. The Lord told Prophet Ezekiel, "I will give them... a new spirit... I will remove their stubborn heart of stone and give them a soft heart of flesh" (Ezekiel 11:19).

A flexible person is happy if he encounters challenges and is likely to view them as an opportunity to improve. He is willing to make changes in his plans and ideas in order to accommodate new perspectives. He can adjust his priorities to suit new realities in order to advance.

A German proverb sums it well, "There is no such a thing as bad weather; only appropriate clothing."

Everyone believed that my sister, Fina, was in the final days of her life. Family members started preparing the home for the likely funeral. From time to time, rumours came up in the community that Fina had died. Relatives, neighbours and friends were always waiting for the final announcement of her expiry, and often turned up to commiserate with the family whenever some spiteful neighbour declared her dead.

In the understanding of the public, the HIV and AIDS disease was an obvious death sentence for any sufferer. People had diagnosed Fina with their eyes and made conclusions about her health status, based on her lifestyle and physical symptoms. Her health had deteriorated gradually as we looked on with the belief that nothing could be done to prevent her death. Most people who had HIV became very thin and were said to have contracted an annihilating disease which came to be referred to as 'slim'.

I travelled from my workplace one afternoon and found a sombre mood at home. Neighbours were gathered in our compound, others seated inside the house while Nyabo and a few of her friends sat by Fina's bedside. They were convinced that she was about to breath her last. I too imagined that everything was beyond human control.

The widespread rumours about my sister suffering from slim, which was incurable, had prompted me to seek more knowledge about this disease. I read books and newspaper articles about HIV and AIDS. I also paid keen attention to anyone talking about the virus. In the due course, I got five ideas about the virus.

One: It was wrong to conclude that someone had slim by merely looking at them. A person needed to take a medical test to confirm that they had acquired the infection. Two: It was possible to control the sickness through effective counselling, proper feeding as well as medication, which was very expensive at the time. Three: Slim was not a death sentence. Someone could still get better and live a normal life.

Four: The disease could not be transmitted through casual contact, therefore, people who had it should not be avoided or condemned. Five: Slim was not a punishment from God against sinners as many people perceived it. Rather, it might be God's way to gauge our compassion towards the suffering.

Jesus taught, "I was hungry and you fed me; thirsty and you gave me a drink; a stranger and you received me; naked and you clothed me; sick and you took care of me; in prison and you visited me… whatever you did for one of the least of my family, you did for me" (Matthew 25:35-40).

When I arrived home, an elder family member had read my mind and took me aside for counselling, "We all know what's happening. She is dying! No need to waste time and resources on treatment. I've seen many of these cases and this is how they die."

I agreed with him in great measure but I also believed the situation was reversible, by the grace of God. I was prepared to try out what I had gathered about such a disease. Amidst protests from the community, I hired a car and arranged to seek medical attention from the AIDS Information Centre in Mbarara, a hundred kilometres away. Everyone said I was wasting time but we arrived safely. Fina received medical tests, counselling and treatment.

Back at home, I broke another tradition. I could bathe and dress up my sister during the initial weeks when she could not help herself, yet many people preferred to keep a distance from her. She was later to recover from the severe condition and lived several more productive years. This changed the perception of our community members about HIV and AIDS. No matter how dire the situation may appear, it is necessary to find creative ways of resolving it.

Faced with severe famine, Abram knew that it was useless to stick to his traditional home. He decided to go to Egypt. Along the way, he realised that the Egyptians might kill him to take his wife Sarai because she was very beautiful.

He told her, "When the Egyptians see you… they will kill me…. Say you are my sister, so that I will be treated well for your sake…" (Genesis 12:10-14).

To register success, it is necessary to think about problems and tasks in creative ways. Flexibility enables a person to cope with the changes in the environment in strategic ways that might also seem submissive. The disciples of Jesus wanted to know who could be the greatest in the kingdom of heaven. Jesus "… placed the child among them… 'Truly I tell you, unless you change and become like little children, you will never enter the kingdom of heaven'" (Matthew 18:2-3).

A flexible person finds it easy to embrace change. British Prime Minister, Wiston Churchill, once said, "There is nothing wrong in change…. To improve is to change, so to be perfect is to have changed often."

When Jesus called his first disciples, the four fishermen, they were not afraid of change. They did not hesitate to grasp the opportunity.

They quickly abandoned their work, "And straightway, they left their nets and followed him.... He went a little farther on and saw two other brothers... he called them; they left their father... and went with Jesus" (Mark 1:14-20).

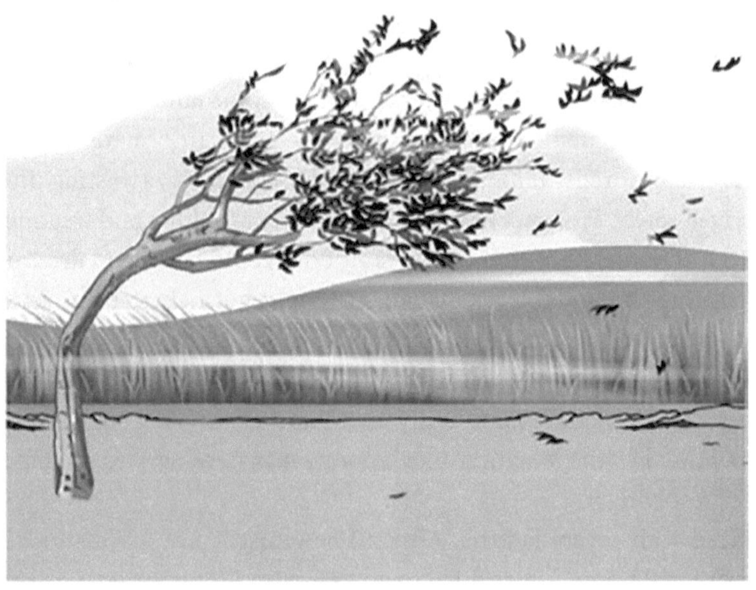

You must be willing to bend if you do not want to break.

Jesus Christ was accused of being too flexible on various occasions. One time, he healed a woman who had been crippled for eighteen years but the leader of the synagogue protested, saying that Jesus should not have done such a thing on the Sabbath.

Jesus asked, "Don't you untie your ox or donkey from its stall on the Sabbath and lead it out for water?" (Luke 13:10-17).

During Jesus Christ's time, the Pharisees and other authorities interpreted religious laws in black and white. People who were understood to be sinners were to be condemned. On the contrary, Jesus taught that spiritual matters should be analysed differently.

He told Nicodemus, a Jewish leader, "For God did not send his Son into the world to condemn the world, but in order that the world might be saved through him" (John 3:17).

Holy as he was, Jesus had a meal at Levi's house together with many tax collectors and sinners. The Pharisees saw him in this environment and expressed disappointment.

Jesus said to them, "It is not the healthy who need a doctor, but the sick. I have not come to call the righteous, but sinners." (Mark 2:15-17).

The disciples picked some corn and the Pharisees accused them of breaking the law by working on the Sabbath. Jesus explained to them the value of the Sabbath, "The Sabbath was made for man, not man for the Sabbath" (Mark 2:27).

In pursuit of excellence, one should not wear a strait jacket and become rigid. One must make a proper assessment of the situation and act accordingly. What works for someone in one environment may not work for another elsewhere.

For example, St Paul says that fasting and eating can serve the same purpose for the different people: "...those who eat anything (all types of food) do so in honour of the Lord…. Those who refuse to eat certain foods do so in honour of the Lord…" (Romans 14:6).

He also adds, "But food does not bring us near to God; we are no worse if we do not eat, and no better if we do" (1 Corinthians 8:8). "Flexibility makes buildings stronger. Imagine what it can do to your soul," said Australian artist, Carlos Barrios.

DO NOT SUBMIT TO MANIPULATION

"A moment came when I sensed that I was about to get a double blessing: a wife and instant riches" - **Author.**

I believed I was about to hit a jackpot! I had been praying and searching for a wife. When I managed to identify one, I quickly arranged a wedding. In the due course, a moment came when I sensed that I was about to get a double blessing: a wife and instant riches.

When I had confirmed the wedding date, I travelled from the small town of Rukungiri, where everyone knew everyone else, to the city of Kampala where no one knew everyone else. In addition to distributing invitation cards to my friends, my mission was to mobilise finances to boost my wedding. I collected quite some money from friends and well-wishers. One day, a former school mate of mine asked me to deliver his invitation card to his premises in the city suburb of Bwaise. I abided, expecting that he would also make a financial contribution towards my wedding. I did not know the exact location of his site, so I started asking some of the residents in the area about my friend's whereabouts. I had hired a motorcycle to travel to that place.

My appearance, speech, mannerisms, dressing and overall contenance betrayed the fact that I was not merely a new character in the area but I had also lately arrived from the countryside. In spite of my rural outlook, I was able to notice that Bwaise was largely a slum and I was the only person wearing a coat and holding a briefcase in the entire community.

I was too different to be treated with friendliness. As I asked for direction from the residents, an innocent-looking young man accosted me with a request.

"Excuse me sir!" he started, "show me the way to Mulago hospital."

I knew that the hospital was situated somewhere in Kampala city but I would not know which direction to take from Bwaise to get there. I imagined the young man had observed that I was the smartest person in the community and, therefore, the only one who could know every part of the city. I felt elated. However, I wanted to be honest to him so that he should not waste more of his and my time discussing the matter.

I confessed to him, "I am new in this area and I don't know most places. Please ask someone else."

The young man fell on his knees and pleaded more earnestly for my assistance. He said he was stranded and might never find his way back home or even faced the greater risk of loss of life if I could not help him. He said I was the only person in the circumstances who had a solution to his dilemma.

I felt pity and started interrogating him about where he was coming from and how he had ended up in the situation he was in. I felt obliged to extend a hand of compassion to the helpless soul kneeling before me. It was the first time ever someone knelt for me.

"A fatal car accident occurred near my home in Mpigi yesterday," he narrated, "and the driver died on the spot. The incident was so serious that it was the main item in the news on the national radio where it was reported that the two injured passengers were evacuated to Mulago hospital. That's why I am going there," he clarified.

Confused, I asked the young man, "Are they your relatives?

Why are going to the hospital?"

"Sir," he replied, "I don't know them. I only picked a valuable item from the site of the accident and decided to bring it to the owners, hopeful that they would refund my fares after receiving their property. I travelled by taxi this morning."

Pulling out of his pocket a glittering, egg-shaped object, the young man went on, "Now I am tired, hungry and hopeless. I know I can't get money for a fare back home. I beg you give me some money for lunch so that I can be able to walk back."

My friends had donated money for my wedding, so I thought I could use a little of it to be generous to this desperate soul. As I attempted to draw money from my pocket, someone intervened in my discussion with the poor youth. He curiously peered at the object in the young man's hand and quickly referred to me as 'a doctor'.

The intruder pulled me by hand, took me aside and said, "Doctor, let me talk to you. This boy is holding a piece of gold. This small item is worth millions of dollars! Please, give him all the money he needs and take it."

Turning to the supplicant, he counselled, "Young man, you will not manage the city life. I don't know where you come from but I see you are in sad state. You might even be arrested if you don't return to your home village. Hand this useless thing to the doctor, take the money he gives you and get away from here."

With the intruder's involvement, my conversation with the dejected young man, which had started from a point of confusion, suddenly mutated into a structured discussion. There was now a mediator to conclude it.

He openly asked how much I was able to raise so that the boy could take it and leave me to sell the 'precious' item to the gold dealers in the city. He grabbed the object from the boy and showed me an inscription on it: *This gold was mined from Southern Tanzania. It is worth $5,000,000.* "You are a very lucky doctor - to be the only person with some money here" the intruder whispered to me. "You will become one of the richest people in Kampala."

At this point, Alex, the friend I had travelled to meet in Bwaise saw me engaged in a conversation with strangers. About five other people had arrived at the scene and I was unconsciously standing in their midst. Alex called out my name and, when I turned to shake hands with him, dragged me from the band of thieves. I survived. To manipulate is to influence someone with a hidden motive.

Every person can be manipulated. Married couples manipulate each other and so do workmates, friends, neighbours, and leaders. In some cases, however, the manipulator is neither dishonest nor destructive such as when a counsellor leads a client to take a helpful decision; or when a spouse sways a partner to make a cost-effective venture.

Where the interaction is sustainably beneficial to both people involved, the influence may be regarded less as manipulation than constructive guidance.

There was an emergency when wine ran out of stock before the bridal ceremony at Cana had reached the highpoint. The mother of Jesus Christ, out of genuine concern, notified him about the crisis, pleading that he should resolve the situation. She also advised the ushers and waiters to abide by the instructions Jesus Christ would give them. Jesus Christ then performed his first miracle by converting raw water into first-class wine.

"...the master of the feast tasted the water now become wine, and did not know where it came from ... (and) called the bridegroom and said to him, 'Everyone serves the good wine first, and when people have drunk freely, then the poor wine. But you have kept the good wine until now'" (John 2:9-10).

The interaction among the players in the episode of Cana was geared solely at finding a solution to the challenge at hand. This means that not all persuasion is manipulation.

As an African proverb proclaims, "The forest hides man's enemies but it is also full of man's medicine."

At the same time, you should be able to discover good intentions in someone's effort to persuade before you can follow their advice.

Always watch out for manipulators among the people you deal with, since Jesus Christ warns, "Beware of false prophets, who come to you in sheep's clothing, but inwardly they are ravening wolves" (Matthew 7:15).

Manipulators do not always have power and talent that is hard to overcome.

Paul also adds, "And no wonder, for even Satan disguises himself as an angel of light" (2 Corinthians 11:14).

The average understanding of manipulation is where a person influences another in an unfair manner, driven by pretence and malice. The manipulator guides his victim towards a harmful condition. The primary factor here is deception and exploitation and involves the promotion of the goals of the manipulative character at the expense of the manipulated individual.

King David committed adultery with Uriah's beautiful wife and hatched a plan to have her fully. He manipulated Uriah by eating and drinking with him and later sent him to deliver a letter to the war commander whom he advised to have Uriah killed.

"In it he wrote, 'Put Uriah out in front where the fighting is fiercest. Then withdraw from him so he will be struck down and die....' some of the men in David's army fell; moreover, Uriah the Hittite died" (2 Samuel 11:15-17).

Fortunately, it is not always true that manipulative people have power and talent that is hard to overcome. Most of them exploit the softness of their victims to advance their motives. People who fall prey to manipulation often have a number of weaknesses. They want to please other people at the cost of their own wellbeing. They are not independent and largely fear to be rejected or abandoned by others.

People who submit to manipulation are individuals who easily get intimidated and can give up their rights and beliefs. They do not have a strong sense of values or ethics to live by. They are ready to surrender their interests as long as it might assure them some comfort, no matter how brief. When you allow another person to manipulate you, you are cooperating with their desire to control your feelings, thoughts, motives and decisions. St. James says that a person who yields to manipulation should also take responsibility for the results; "But each person is tempted when he is lured and enticed by his own desire. Then desire when it has conceived gives birth to sin, and sin when it is fully grown brings death" (James 1:14-15).

The serpent in the Garden of Eden capitalised on Eve's appetite to upset the couple's favour with God. The Lord had told them that if they ate of the forbidden tree, they would die. However, the serpent contradicted God and manipulated Eve to doubt God's word.

"'You will not certainly die', the serpent said to the woman. 'For God knows that when you eat from it, your eyes will be opened, and you will be like God, knowing good and evil'" (Genesis 3:4-5).

In the end, they ate from the forbidden tree; and this decision was much more than Adam and Eve just being hungry. Neither was it because God did not provide the necessary information to the couple about the dangers of doing such a thing. They simply were too greedy to stick to the moral standards set by God. When God demanded answers, Adam simply blamed Eve who in turn blamed the serpent. The couple was punished ultimately.

If you surrender to manipulation and end up in trouble as a result, you must blame yourself and acknowledge that you contributed to your situation. You gain nothing to blame the manipulator when the damage is already done. The tragedy is that many people seem unready to remain morally upright when temptations arise in form of physical, social or economic difficulties.

Worse still, some people might attempt to justify their failures by attributing them to God.

St James provides a very good answer, "Let no one say when he is tempted, 'I am being tempted by God'; … He does not tempt any one. But each one is tempted when he is seduced under his own desires" (James 1:13-14).

Scripture shows that it is not only possible but also profitable for a person to resist manipulation against all odds. The most known story is of Job who was greatly tried. Satan subjected him to extreme suffering so that he could reject God but Job could not yield.

Job lost all his property, children, servants and health. His friends and family coerced him intensely to curse God in order to secure some relief but he still refused. His integrity remained intact and all his blessings were eventually restored and multiplied. He had lost all his seven sons, three daughters, seven thousand sheep, three thousand camels, five hundred oxen and five hundred she-asses.

"…..the Lord blessed the latter days of Job more than his earlier ones; he had fourteen thousand sheep, and six thousand camels, and a thousand yoke of oxen, and a thousand she-asses. He had also seven sons and three daughters…. Job lived a hundred and forty years, and saw his sons and his sons' sons, even four generations" (Job 42:10-16).

Lazarus tolerated his misery as a destitute. When he died, the angels carried him into Abraham's bosom. When his rich neighbour died and went to hell, he attempted to manipulate Abraham to use his privileged position and send Lazarus to mitigate his pain by dropping some water from his finger to his tongue (Luke 16:19-31). At this point, it was hard to manipulate the situation.

The Magi arrived in Bethlehem and believed that they would be able to get useful information about the birth of Jesus Christ from the palace of the king, Herod. They expected the entire province to be excited about the advent of the Divine king but this was not the case. Instead, Herod was uneasy about the news and tried to coach the Magi to become spies on whose evidence he would base to kill Jesus. With the help of an angel, however, the Magi were able detect the king's manipulation and the baby was safe since they did not return to Herod.

"When King Herod heard this he was disturbed, and all Jerusalem with him…. Then Herod called the Magi secretly… sent them to Bethlehem and said, 'Go and make a careful search for the child. As soon as you have found him, report to me so that I too may go and worship him'. And having been warned in a dream not to go back to Herod, they returned to their country by another route" (Matthew 2:3-12)

A manipulative person has a way of twisting your thoughts, actions or desires to suit his hidden motives. He can transfer his own guilt onto you, make you begin to doubt yourself, and to imagine that what he wants is what you also want. The manipulator destroys your independence in decision making and controls your thought processes and actions, thus you behave as though you are remote- controlled. If you are not careful, someone can manipulate you into things that might destroy your health, character, reputation and future.

WHEN IN DOUBT, ASK

The Greek have a Proverb: 'Wonder is the beginning of wisdom.'

Similarly, Bertrand Russell, a British philosopher has said, "In all affairs, it's a healthy thing now and then to hang a question mark on the things you have long taken for granted."[7] Uganda conducted national elections for delegates to participate in the making of the new National Constitution in 1994. Every county required a delegate while a district elected a woman to participate on the affirmative action platform. It was quite a competitive election whereby contenders spent sleepless nights visiting the electors to persuade them.

To conduct public rallies, however, no candidate was expected to move alone. The Electoral Commission attempted to make the process transparent. This was before the new government slipped into blatant electoral fraud. All the residents in a parish would converge in one place where all the candidates would present their various manifestos, one after another, before the voters would raise questions.

The youngest of the contenders was the government favourite and clearly the most popular among the voters. Sebo and his entire family supported him. When he spoke, everyone cheered. He pledged, among others, that Kajara County would become a model constituency during his one-year tenure as a delegate to the Constituent Assembly.

"Vote for me and you will never regret!" he promised. "I will ensure that there is clean water in every home. Our schools will become the best in the country. You deserve a hospital and I am going to ensure you get it very soon. I will improve the state of our roads so that you can transport your

---

7   Bertrand Russell (1872-1970).

crops to the markets. I will find markets for all your crops and poverty will become history in your homes," he declared as the crowd chanted praises for him.

He concluded, "You will be my witnesses when delegates from other areas start coming to this county to learn how to develop their own constituencies."

When time for feedback from the audience came, Sebo was among the first to raise their hands and got an opportunity to put a question to a specific candidate. The norm was that a voter would question the wisdom of the candidate he did not support. Hence, Sebo who was a known supporter of the popular candidate was expected either extol him as a godsend or query the pledges of his rivals.

Sebo stated, "I have listened to the wonderful ideas of the candidate who spoke first. If he delivers as promised, we shall be the happiest people in this country," he added as the crowd drowned his speech with handclaps as there was no microphone.

"My question is," he went on, "we have elected leaders for a long time but none has achieved what you are promising us - neither in this constituency nor elsewhere. How will you manage? Are you God?"

The multitude shouted uncontrollably, this time cursing and jeering.

The candidate was not allowed to give an answer. "Don't answer such a question," someone yelled.

"It is a stupid question. Ignore him," another screamed. "He hates our government," another cried out.

"He is anti-development," some voices chorused.

The candidate, in the end, declined to answer the question and thanked the people for noticing the obvious malice. He advised them to continue supporting his vision to make the county prosperous.

On the day of elections, the popular candidate was declared the legitimate winner. He went to the Constituent Assembly and was re-elected thereafter as a Member of Parliament. Surprisingly, little, if anything, changed. Sebo was right after all.

In Christianity, some people use Scripture to discourage believers from asking questions about God.

They cite John 20:29 where Jesus said to Thomas, "Blessed are they who have not seen and yet have believed."

However, Jesus was always willing to answer people's questions and did not categorise their quest for Divine truths as sinning.

Faith in God must not be 'blind faith'! God is the author of all the faculties of your body and soul. By giving you a brain, a heart, and all organs that mark you as a human being, God desired that you should put these gifts to wise use.

He who asks may be a fool for a moment. He who does not ask stays a fool forever

In fact, Jesus Christ instructs believers to ask from God; "Ask and you will receive…" (Matthew 7:7).

The story of Zechariah and Elizabeth is quite edifying. When the Angel announced to Zechariah that Elizabeth, his wife, would get pregnant and give birth to a boy, he responded with a question. "How can I believe this?" Zechariah said, "I am an old man and my wife is elderly too" (Luke 1:18).

As a punishment for his disbelief, Zechariah became dumb until the Angel's proclamation was fulfilled. Elizabeth became pregnant and bore a boy. Does this affirm that asking questions is wrong? No. Would God punish you in the same way as he did to Zechariah for asking questions? Yes, only if you ask with total lack of faith.

The forefather of all believers, Abraham, had amazing faith. Yet he sought more information from God who pledged that Sarah would produce a son.

Said Abraham, "Will a son be born to a man a hundred years old? And can Sarah who is ninety have a child?" (Genesis 17:17).

In the same vein, Abraham's wife, Sarah, found it odd to learn that she would become pregnant, thus she asked, "Now that I am old and worn…. Am I really going to have a child…?" (Genesis 18:12- 13).

When this promise delayed, Abraham again asked, "My Lord,

Yahweh, where are your promises?" (Genesis 15:2).

He further sought assurance that he would get the promised inheritance, "My Lord, how am I to know that it shall be mine?" When Abram referred to the Almighty, he got a favourable answer. A son, Isaac, was born to him when he was already "a hundred years old" (Genesis 21:1-7).

To ask God means to seek His wisdom through prayers, knowing that He is the provider of all our needs and does not disappoint. Any difficult condition you may encounter is the perfect opportunity to put to God all your unanswered questions in prayer. To ask is to express your humility and eagerness to learn; and it shows the confidence you have in the person you ask.

Scripture says, "Now this is the confidence that we have in Him, that if we ask anything according to His will, He hears us" (1 John 5:14-15).

Questions always arise whenever complex situations emerge and, if you ask God in prayer, you get the appropriate answers and solutions. Manoah's wife was barren and the couple deeply desired a child. One day, the Angel communicated to them that the barren woman would conceive and produce a boy. They were excited about the news but felt inadequate about what to do next.

The couple sought clarification and guidance thus; "I pray you, Lord, that the man of God… may come again to us and teach us how to bring up the boy who is to be born" (Judges 13:8).

Manoah essentially demanded more information because he believed and trusted in God. In the end, a powerful son, Samson, was born.

In another case, when Yahweh appeared to Gideon and told him that he was chosen to save the Israelites from the hands of Midianites, Gideon responded with a question. "…but how can I save Israel? My family is the lowliest in my tribe and I am the least in the family of my father" (Judges 6:25).

God noticed Gideon's fear and fortified him with illustrative signs. With a small army, Gideon ably conducted successful military campaigns. Mary, the mother of Jesus Christ, is seen as an epithet of humility, faith and obedience to God. At the time of the annunciation, however, she did not understand the message of Angel Gabriel at once and she took courage to pose a question.

The Angel told Mary, "You shall conceive and bear a son."

Mary's immediate response was, "How can this be since I am a virgin?" (Luke 1:31-34).

Angel Gabriel then offered a full account of how God had planned the Saviour's birth (Luke 1:35-37).

During his ministry, Jesus Christ contended with questions many times. When he requested for drinking water at Jacob's well in the Samaritan town, he was only interrogated.

The Samaritan woman wondered, "How is it that you, a Jew, should ask me, a Samaritan and a woman, for a drink?" (John 4:9). The woman asked because she saw Jesus as a Jew, and Jews hated Samaritans. Moreover, just talking to a woman in public was socially proscribed. The Samaritan woman was shocked that although Jesus was supposed to know the rules, he went ahead to ask for a drink. In the course of the argument, the woman realised that she interacted with the Messiah. Jesus did not judge her for asking questions.

There is also a rich man who, on his first encounter with Jesus Christ, posed a question that culminated into a duteous exploration (Matthew 19: 16-22).

The rich man asked, "What good work must I do to receive eternal life?" Jesus replied, "If you want to enter eternal life, keep the commandments."

The man went on, "Which commandments?" and Jesus mentioned the commandments.

The man said, "I have kept all these commandments. What do I still lack?"

Jesus told him, "… go, sell all that you possess and give the money to the poor."

One may imagine that a man who kept all the commandments did not have anything to ask about his faith. Yet when he asked, he discovered that he was not perfect and there was a lot more he needed to do.

The conversation between Jesus and the rich young man touched the disciples. The man was asked to give away his property to become worthy of eternal life. This prompted Peter to seek an answer about the status of all the apostles who had already abandoned all the social and economic trappings to follow Jesus.

Peter said, "You see we have given up everything to follow you.

What then will be there for us?"

Jesus said, "You … will receive much more … and eternal life in the world to come" (Luke 18:30).

Jesus Christ was not disappointed that Peter, a senior apostle, could put across a question whereas they had lived with him for a considerable duration; neither that all the other apostles disassociated themselves from Peter's question. God knows that you do not have the capacity to comprehend Divine truths at a glance. It is important to seek answers from Him in all situations. A problem arises when you experience difficult conditions and begin to challenge God with questions, blaming and accusing Him, instead of asking to be fortified to overcome the problems. When God called Prophet Jeremiah, he assured him of authority and victory over nations and kingdoms. The prophet accepted the task, imagining that he would just talk and people would immediately abide by his word.

Jeremiah was upset when, instead, the people consistently ridiculed and plotted to kill him. Although they were wicked, they were also prosperous and Jeremiah wondered how God could allow that to happen.

He asked, "Why are the wicked so prosperous? Why do dishonest people succeed? (Jeremiah 12:1).

When Jeremiah asked, God alerted him that what he was going through was minor, compared to what was to come.

He said, "If you can't even stand up in open country, how you will manage in the jungle of the Jordan?" (Jeremiah 12:5)

When you ask, please wait for the answer. Give God a chance to give an appropriate answer since he understands the motives behind your questions. As a result, God's answers may be different from what you expect or desire but they will certainly teach you more.

The Chinese say, "He who asks a question may be a fool for five minutes; he who asks no questions stays a fool forever."

MAINTAIN YOUR INTEGRITY

"Better is a poor man who walks in his integrity than a rich man who is crooked in his ways" **(Proverbs 28:6).**

Integrity is not a matter of social status a person has attained but an individual's interior disposition, which other people can recognise, nonetheless. An African proverb fittingly illustrates that 'character is like pregnancy which the possessor cannot hide with bare hands'.

Uganda attempted to embrace democratic governance in 1996 after the new National Constitution was adopted the previous year. The incumbent President was nominated alongside a couple of other candidates to contest for the highest office in the land. It was during the same year I graduated and got a job as a school teacher. I was a strong admirer of the President and eagerly joined throngs of supporters when he campaigned at Rukungiri district stadium. As usual, he charmed us with assurances of progress in the economic, health, education, justice and other sectors. He concluded by declaring that there was no need to listen to any of his competitors, so no one should show up when they would hold rallies in the same location.

It sounded like a joke but when the leading opposition candidate visited the district, the police and other security officials locked the stadium and sent away many people who wished to attend. Elections were to be held in a few months, first for the President and thereafter for Parliament.

I was privileged to be recruited as a Presiding Officer for one of the Polling Stations near my home. I was going to manage the voting at Mahwa Primary School Station. When we opened the station on Election Day, many voters queued up and cast their polls very well. By mid-morning, however, suspicious characters started lining up to vote.

Some were underage children carrying voters' cards of their deceased relatives while others held cards of people who had migrated and settled in other locations. Some brought cards of sick neighbours who were unable to get to the polling station as well as those of people who had travelled and would only return to the village after the elections.

Some people who had already voted from neighbouring polling stations lined up at my polling station to vote again, boasting that they had been allowed to do the same elsewhere. I could not allow any of these characters to vote as I had to follow the rules, a handbook of which I had on my table. I was only shocked to see the agents of the incumbent President complaining against the act of sending away people who were not eligible to vote. They argued that they had been assured that anyone who could turn up at the polling station would have to cast a vote, even though they were not qualified to do so. They went ahead and complained to a government minister who was also a voter in the same constituency. "Our Polling Station has been messed up," someone told him, "because the Presiding Officer is very strict!"

Whereas the principle of 'One Man, One Vote' was the guiding standard, there was an unwritten rule that well-known supporters of the incumbent President should vote as many times as they chose at any polling station. In the same vein, ineligible voters who were believed to support the incumbent President had 'a right' to vote.

As I did my work, I had, at the back of my mind, what St Paul says, "For we aim at what is honourable… in the Lord's sight but also in the sight of man" (2 Corinthians 8:21).

I refused to participate in the fraud; the practice was different at my station. I never allowed multiple voting, sent away people without voters' cards as well as everyone with a card that was clearly not theirs. Fortunately, I knew almost everyone who was registered to vote at this polling station in my birthplace.

My behaviour angered the supporters of the incumbent President who started to label me as a promoter of multi-party politics, banned in the country at that time. This was a serious accusation as it was illegal to do so under the newly inaugurated national constitution.

The Government Minister, who was also from the same County, came to see what was happening at my polling station. He had received the complaints about me. After a little briefing by the campaign agents, he walked into the polling arena without permission. He made a mistake because he was neither a returning officer nor did he hold any official role in the electoral process.

Better is a poor man who walks in his integrity than a rich man who is crooked in his ways

He inquired, "I have heard that you are denying people the chance to vote. Why?"

"We are only sending away people who are not eligible to vote, sir," I replied.

He probed, "How do you tell someone is ineligible to vote?".

"Some individuals have presented voters' cards of people who, we know, have died," I explained. "Others are underage but they have brought cards that belong to their parents who are now absent from this village."

"That's not a problem," the Minister said. "It's a long time since people last voted, so they are excited! Allow them to vote as they want."

"It's against the electoral guidelines," I said showing him the booklet. "During the recent training on election management, the Returning Officer told us to follow these guidelines," I added.

"Young man," he shouted, "Is your head working properly? Who is a Returning Officer? It's our government that appointed him, so we are in charge of these elections, not him," he stressed.

I knew the Minister was trying to mislead me, so I answered, "For me, I am working as I was told."

The Minister was clearly angry. He walked briskly towards his car. It was as though he had gone to collect a document that was superior to the guidelines I was using. Instead, he drove away, sending a cloud of dust into the sky.

The bystanders had expected me to tremble at the sight of the Minister. In their ordinary understanding, the elections belonged to 'the government' as the Minister stated. Therefore, the community members were only favoured to participate by casting ballots and hence had a duty to imagine the wishes of 'the government' and act accordingly.

They did not view themselves as part of the government. It was not only strange but a sign of gross indiscipline that 'a boy' who had just left school should talk to the Minister as I did. Nevertheless, scores of ineligible voters who had hoped that impunity would prevail started leaving the queue, noticing my determination to prevent fraud.

Referring to me, someone said, "Such a person should be blacklisted! He should never be allowed to participate in any future election as a polling official."

"Yes! He is spoilt. He is undermining the government," several people supplemented.

The polling ended and everyone returned home, many disappointed with me. Some people even complained to my father about my behaviour at the polling station. If he were not a strong character, he would have apologised on my behalf.

Then, I was surprised when the next elections came only two months later. Three candidates contested to represent Kajara County in the National Assembly. It was such a tight race that the Electoral Commission had to consult the candidates about how the voting process would be structured. The consensus was that the three candidates would each nominate one person per polling station to be appointed as a polling official so that none would take an unfair advantage to win the elections. They were concerned that officials who managed the recent elections had promoted cheating and, if allowed to perform the same role, would thwart the will of the people. The Presidential elections had been such a sham due to their dubious conduct. Individually, the candidates would be uncomfortable if they knew that electoral fraud similar to what had occurred during the Presidential elections might be upheld.

The candidates' agents had to identify trustable persons to be appointed in accordance with an agreement reached with the Electoral Commission. I was nominated by all the three camps!

"He cannot allow anyone to cheat even if the candidate does have a representative at the polling station," one of the agents suggested during a consultative meeting. "Do you remember how he managed the Presidential elections? He acted in the most straightforward way," someone said of me.

The psalmist points out that a person of integrity is one who exudes such reliability as to be consistent, honest and kind in all conditions. Such an individual would not sacrifice standard values for social expedience or discard esteemed morals for personal comfort.

"He who walks blamelessly and does what is right and speaks truth in his heart... and does no evil to his neighbour... who honours those who fear the Lord; who swears to his own heart and does not change.... He who does these things shall never be moved" (Psalms 15:1-5).

A person who steals a coin from a stranger is deficient in integrity as much as one who loots state resources from the taxpayers. Most of the grand corruption scandals on record have been committed by people who started by stealing pencils and rubbers from classmates at school, before they graduated into notorious plunderers.

Jesus Christ says, "Whoever can be trusted with very little can also be trusted with much, and whoever is dishonest with very little will also be dishonest with much" (Luke 16:10).

A student of integrity would study hard to pass instead of resorting to cheating on a school test. A worker with integrity does not cut corners or slack off instead of paying serious attention to the job. A woman of integrity would not indulge on expensive presents or expect other people to pay for her when on an outing. A man of integrity would not drive home drunk and ignore the welfare of his family and other people.

A renowned clinical psychologist, Barbara Killinger (McGill- Queen's, 2007) in '*Integrity: Doing the Right Thing for the Right Reason*', refers to integrity as a personal choice… and predictably consistent commitment to honour moral, ethical, spiritual and artistic values and principles.

The word 'integrity' springs from 'integer' *(Latin)*, which means 'whole' or 'complete'. Acting with honour and truthfulness are some of the basic tenets in a person with integrity. To have integrity means to act with honesty at all times, guided by the standard morals, values or beliefs that are considered desirable for a decent character.

In this commentary, we focus on a few biblical episodes to illustrate some of the key indicators of integrity, which include reliability, transparency, morality, contentment, self-discipline and decisiveness.

Morality is the bedrock of integrity. Genesis 39:7-23 shows that when he lived at the palace in Egypt, the Pharaoh's wife approached Joseph for sex. Someone else would have felt privileged to be 'loved' by the king's wife, immoral as it would be.

However, Joseph flatly rejected the temptation, "….he refused and said '…my master… has put everything that he has in my charge… except yourself, because you are his wife. How then can I do this great wickedness…?"

Every day, the woman persuaded Joseph but he would not listen to her. "…she caught him by his garment, saying; 'Lie with me'. But he left his garment in her hand and fled …."

Out of malice, she told Pharaoh that Joseph had attempted to rape her "…he blazed with anger… took Joseph and put him in the Royal Prison… but Yahweh was with him."

As one African proverb goes, 'you must observe the character of your guest before killing the chicken'. Joseph demonstrated such a high moral standard that he eventually rose to the rank of a Prime Minister in Egypt shortly after his discharge from prison.

Acts 5:1-11 shows that integrity is not compatible with selfishness; rather, it thrives on truth and transparency. "…a man named Ananias; together with his wife Sapphira… sold a piece of property… he kept back part of the money for himself, but brought the rest and put it at the apostles' feet. Then Peter said, '… you have lied to the Holy Spirit…. You have not lied just to human beings but to God."

When Ananias heard this, he fell down and died... later his wife came in… she fell down … and died (Acts 5:1-11). With integrity, the severe punishment which the couple suffered would have been avoidable.

In one of her speeches, Michelle Obama, the First Lady of the United States (2009-2016), has said, "We learned about honesty and integrity; that the truth matters… that you don't take shortcuts or play by your own set of rules… and success doesn't count unless you earn it fair and square." A person with integrity also relishes contentment. One day, Esau returned from the field and, since he was famished, quickly traded his rank as firstborn for food.

Therefore, he said, "Since I am to die (of hunger) soon, what good is my right as firstborn to me…." (Genesis 25:31-35).

Being a firstborn was not only a position of privilege but he was clearly not in danger of death from hunger. His greedy and weak personality largely shaped his behaviour.

Such an attitude contradicts the notion, "Man does not live by bread alone" (Matthew 4:4).

As he scorned his birth right, Esau paid heavily when he lost the decisive parental blessing to Jacob, the younger son. One wonders what was in Esau's mind as he conceded his birth right for a teeming bowl of stew. In our day, Esau typifies people who are willing to sell their souls to earn temporary relief; which often brings suffering to both an individual and community.

On the other hand, Jacob was primarily disadvantaged. He was not a firstborn. He was not as adventurous and talented as Esau was. He was not a high achiever, nor did his father favour him. He was only able to occupy the family gap created by his superior brother as a result of his wanton appetite.

Mahatma Gandhi says, "There are seven things that will destroy us: Wealth without work; Pleasure without conscience; Knowledge without character; Religion without sacrifice; Politics without principle; Science without humanity; Business without ethics."

Self-discipline is also a mark of integrity. Food and drink are major items of gratification but Scripture shows that Daniel refused to defile himself with the king's food, or with the wine that he drank. The chief of the eunuchs warned Daniel about the dangers that would result from his apparent contempt for the king's offers. He said, "I fear my lord the king, who assigned your food and your drink; for why should he see that you were in worse condition than the youths who are of your own age? So you would endanger my head with the king."

Then Daniel said to the steward, "Test your servants for ten days; let us be given vegetables to eat and water to drink (Daniel 1:8-20).

Later, God rewarded Daniel's integrity not only with the subdual of the lions' appetites when he was thrown into their den but also with the reputation as the king's favourite governor thereafter. Like Joseph in Egypt, Daniel earned a higher reputation than his contemporaries who submitted to manipulation.

An American researcher on relationships and personal growth, Barbara De Angelis, says, "Living with integrity means: Not settling for less than what you know you deserve…. Asking for what you want and need from others. Speaking your truth, even though it might create conflict or tension; behaving in ways that are in harmony with your values; making choices based on what you believe…"[8]

Success demands that one has to seek God's help but, at the same time, be able to take timely decisions. Integrity therefore goes with decisiveness. As Jesus Christ called his apostles, one of them said, "I will follow You, Lord; but first permit me to say good- bye to those at home." Probably, the apostle was hesitating to take a serious decision.

But Jesus said to him, "No one who puts his hand to the plough and looks back is fit for the kingdom of God" (Luke 9:61-62)."

St Paul makes a case for integrity thus, "Finally, brothers, whatever is true, whatever is honourable, whatever is just, whatever is pure, whatever is lovely, whatever is commendable, if there is any excellence, if there is anything worthy of praise, think about these things" (Philippians 4:8).

---

8   Adapted from www.InformativeQuotes.com.

THE VALUE OF SHARING

"Those who bring sunshine into the lives of others cannot keep it from themselves," says Sir James Matthew Barrie, a Scottish author and dramatist.

Whatever 'little' resources are available to an individual can be enough to benefit his neighbour as well. When you share with others, you multiply your chances to get more and more returns.

Said Jesus, "Give and it will be given to you... for by your standard of measure, it will be measured to you in turn" (Luke 6:38). When I completed school and entered the world of employment, I believed there was nothing to stand in my way to success in life. All I needed was education and I had attained it. I felt I was on the top of the world and all doors would open wherever I could knock.

My mind told me that I was the best teacher ever to qualify from Uganda's education system. At this point, I did not think I needed anyone's help to live happily. Within a month, I had secured a job at Immaculate Heart Girls' School as a teacher.

However, the school did not have sufficient facilities to provide accommodation for all the teachers, especially new ones. This was a blow since I had anticipated that it was a big school, able to cater for all the basic needs of a new teacher. I had not yet started working and, therefore, did not have money to rent a room outside the school.

In the midst of the crisis, a friend of mine, Frank, advised me to talk to his father who had a vacant room at their home which was a little more than a kilometre away from the school. I contacted his father, suggesting that he allowed me to occupy the room as I looked for the money to sort the rent. When I told him that I intended to stay at his house briefly as I looked for another room in the trading centre so that I could access electricity, the man offered to accommodate me at no cost for such a short time.

The following term, the head teacher arranged that I should start living within the school, sharing a house with Mr Ngira, a teacher who had just got a wife. She, nonetheless, noted that it all depended on Mr Ngira's willingness to accept me in the house. During my short time in the school, I had gathered that any teacher who was married was entitled to occupy a schoolhouse privately with his family.

Mr Ngira lived in the house with his wife, a maid and another relative. Occasionally, he also hosted visitors who included friends, in-laws and relatives, hence he would utilise all the rooms in the house from time to time. I did not expect him to agree to share a house with a person he did not know well, moreover when he knew the rules. To my amazement, he accepted to share.

I was rescued from paying rent for a second time. I could only spend on food. I was not a good cook and always got bored with long processes of preparing meals. I would have desired to take my meals from a restaurant but I did not have money. Therefore, I often prepared a quick evening meal by frying rice and tomatoes or I slept hungry sometimes.

Another teacher, Willison, lived next door and his wife noted that I was not having regular meals. Whereas I did not consider that I was in a pitiable condition, Joy was very concerned. She discussed it with her husband who sanctioned that she could give me part of their family meals, sometimes. On several occasions, Joy surprised me with mouth-watering dishes of chicken, salads and other foodstuffs unusual to me.

Time for me to quit teaching came eight years after I had enteredtheprofession. Ihad, duringcollegedays, vowedthat Iwould not teach for more than ten years if I did not become a head teacher within the same period. In a bid to live to my word, I unsuccessfully applied for a job in a non-governmental organisation. When I got a letter of regret, I followed up and learnt that the only option to get into the organisation was to work as a volunteer.

I decided to become one. Yet it required a lot of expenditure since I had to shift from a free house and a salaried job and relocate to Kampala city where the cost of living was very high. I needed to pay for the daily fares, meals and accommodation to do a job for no pay.

Once again, a friend, Sunday, took me into his room where he had a single bed and a chair. We shared the small space. At night, I would place my mattress on the floor in order to sleep, only to fold and place it in the corner of the room every morning before heading to work. Wherever I went, people were ready to share.

Wealth is not how much is in your bank account but what is in your heart

Sharing is similar to planting. Just as we fling a seed into the ground to receive back multiple seeds at harvest time, so it is with everything we give; including money, assets, emotions, prayers or time. We always reap a harvest on whatever we give.

In one of his epistles, St Paul states, "Do not be deceived: God cannot be mocked. A man reaps what he sows" (Galatians 6:7).

The earth is endowed with vast natural resources at the disposal of humanity. Unfortunately, many communities around the world are plagued with poverty and scarcity to such a magnitude that some people simply cannot get what to eat. As rulers and their compradors swim in luxurious wealth, whole peasant families and communities sink deeper into abjection.

It is clear that the problem of poverty is not that the poor are reluctant to apply themselves adequately to improve their status. Rather, exploitative social and economic systems that exist deny people access to the fruits of their sweat.

Jesus teaches that national wealth is not meant to whet the appetites of the people who are privileged. One time, nightfall came when Jesus was ministering to a large audience. His disciples asked him to send away the crowds as they believed they did not have sufficient food for all of them. They told Jesus, "…you should send the people away… to buy themselves something to eat…. If we are to feed them, we need two hundred silver coins to go and buy enough bread" (Mark 6:36-37).

Jesus did not agree and replied, "Have the people seated together in groups" (Mark 6:39; Mark 8:6; John 6:10).

In one incident, Jesus Christ fed four thousand people with only seven loaves of bread and a few fish. In another case, he fed five thousand men on five loaves and two fish. They all ate and were satisfied, leaving enough leftovers to feed another crowd.

Preaching on the miracle of multiplication, Pope Francis has said, "… if there is a will, what we have never ends. On the contrary, it abounds and does not get wasted."

It is the absence of the spirit of sharing, other than the lack of resources, which is enhancing the catastrophe of poverty and hunger in the world.

Whereas Jesus was able to perform the miracles of multiplication, the mentality of the apostles appears to have been formed by selfishness. Their demand that Jesus should send away the rest of the people resembles the current attitude of the elites who seem to claim exclusive rights over public resources.

Privileged individuals often take hefty payments while powerless civil servants such as teachers and health workers still yearn for minimal salaries. Worse still, every century that passes leaves in its trails more and more citizens who are sweating daily to survive.

It is gravely ironical and scandalous that at the time when world economies boast of unprecedented development indicators, the poor continue to wallow in misery. About a billion people worldwide reportedly continue to experience hunger in the twenty- first century.

"There is no humiliation more abusive than hunger," says Pranab Mukherjee, who assumed office in 2012 as the thirteenth President of the Republic of India.

Therefore, the teachers, health workers, security officers and other labourers need not go on strike to merit a decent pay. Children need not kneel or toil to enjoy the essentials of life. Peasants need not di of hunger to attract the attention of 'charity' institutions. Women need not to tussle to realise their right to inherit family estates or access gainful employment.

Prophet Elijah asked a poor widow for a drink and food. She told him that she had no bread left except very little flour and oil; hardly enough to satisfy her and her son for a single meal. She was worried about the food security of her household and was clearly alarmed that Elijah insisted she should use the flour and oil to make a cake for him.

Luckily, she was able to modify her mind-set quickly enough to accommodate the needs of a stranger. The result was fantastic. "The jar of flour was not emptied nor did the jug of oil…" (1 Kings 17:11-16)

God has endowed the earth sufficiently for the fulfilment of all people. If we do not know how to listen to the word of God, we cannot solve our urgent problems especially fair distribution of wealth and tearing down of barriers to justice and equal privileges. Proper guidance on mutual utilisation of resources is highly documented in the Scripture.

During his mission as the Lord's forerunner, John the Baptist preached thus, "If you have two shirts, give one to the poor. If you have food, share it with those who are hungry" (Luke 3:11).

Jesus Christ further elevated the value of sharing of resources. He said that it would be considered greatly at the time of the final judgement.

"When the Son of Man comes… he will separate people one from another as a shepherd separates the sheep from the goats… the sheep on his right, but the goats on the left. Then the King will say to those on his right, 'Come, you who are blessed by my Father, inherit the kingdom …. For I was hungry and you gave me food, I was thirsty and you gave me drink, I was a stranger and you welcomed me" (Matthew 25:31-46).

Sharing therefore should be a hands-on human experience. It is not enough to wish others well without practically tackling the troubles afflicting them. St James teaches that wishful behaviour is essentially useless.

"If a brother or sister is poorly clothed and lacking in daily food, and one of you says to them, 'Go in peace, be warmed and filled,' without giving them the things needed for the body, what good is that? So also faith by itself, if it does not have works, is dead" (James 2:14-17).

ACT WITH COURAGE

"Be strong and take courage, all you who hope in the Lord" (Psalms 31:24).

Someone has described courage as a state of mind that enables a person to rise above fear, pain, danger or hardship. Physical courage is the ability to overcome fears of possible bodily harm, while mental courage is the ability to resist worries whether they are real or imagined. Moral courage is the capacity to do the right thing in spite of popular hostility. A courageous person is willing to stand up when other people want him or her to sit down. Life presents infinite opportunities for success. However, opportunities often come shrouded in what may appear as unsafe conditions which only a person with courage is able to tolerate. People sometimes fail to make it in life when they do not recognise that success is not a preserve of a few, but an entitlement for everyone. The only thing required is the courage to pursue and grab success, irrespective of the threats it may seem to camouflage in. Erica Jong, author of *Fear of Flying*, says, "Everyone has talent.

What's rare is the courage to follow it to the dark places where it leads."

Three months after suspending my teaching career, I got a worrying offer. While I broke out of the school system into a non- governmental organisation, I still felt and acted like the teacher I was. I had joined a profession clearly different from what I studied.

I had not yet read enough literature about my new work. I was fumbling to use a computer where younger boys and girls, fresh from university, performed with dazzling precision. Above all, I was not an authentic employee but a volunteer in the organisation and I still nursed nostalgia for handling students.

One day, the Director invited me to his office and asked, "Are you able to seize a challenging opportunity?"

"What opportunity?" I replied.

"I have received a request from our Head Office in Nairobi to nominate a person who has sufficient experience in the work we do to help in setting up a new organisation in the Republic of Tanzania," he said, "and I wanted to find out if you would be interested to grasp this opportunity."

He explained that the assignment would last a year, with only one chance to visit my family and no salary but a little stipend to cater for basic needs like accommodation, food, communication and healthcare. Starting from scratch, I would generate and submit a work plan for approval by the Head Office, set up and manage the national secretariat, recruit members to constitute both General Assembly and Executive Board, identify funding opportunities and establish networks with strategic agencies.

I did not understand what the Director was telling me as I knew I was the most unlikely candidate for such a task. I was sure I lacked almost everything required for the job he described as I was still struggling to learn many things. At best, I thought he was teasing me.

I had some ambitions and that was the reason I ventured into a non-governmental organisation but I believed I could only go so far. What the Director outlined was clearly so remote to my dreams that, by the end of our discussion, I had concluded he was looking for a way to dismiss me from the organisation. I suspected that I had failed to perform to the required standard and I was being edged out of the system tactfully.

"I understand that this would be a challenging task for you," he said. "Think about it and give me feedback by the end of next week."

I left the office confused. My commitment to change my career was tested. Yes, I had been glad to quit the teaching job but I was also willing to bite only what I could chew. What the Director was suggesting was far beyond my imagination! Yet I had to give him feedback within a week.

The solution was to consult my friends about it. The first person I shared my challenge with appeared to joke about it.

"You are lucky, you man. You are going to become a diplomat!" he observed, showing little interest in discussing the details.

Other friends, nevertheless, were nearly unanimous as they offered critical standpoints. They pointed out various risks.

"You have a young wife," one pointed out, "so you cannot make a mistake of staying away from her for a year. She'll be taken away!" This friend brought up a matter I had not thought about previously. I always took my wife for granted, believing that she was married 'for better or worse' as we vowed at our wedding three years earlier. In his view, however, she was a person who could run away, given a chance.

Another friend stated the subject almost in similar terms, "Remember how hard you've worked to start a family and the trouble you will face if it breaks down. You have to value your family above anything else."

"We all want money but you should not pursue it at the cost of your life," counselled another friend. "How can you do such work which you've never done before - moreover in a foreign country?" he added.

When I had left the Director's office, I was afraid and anxious at once. Afraid because I perceived the mission to be too big for me. Anxious because I desired to surmount such a challenge. Little by little, his words had sunk into my psyche like a charm. His pose and news had stuck to my mind like a Divine revelation. Like Mary at the birth of Jesus, I 'treasured all these things and pondered them at heart' (Luke 2:19).

Whenever I consulted, therefore, I was looking for a simple endorsement from a friend or two in order to take a step. Whereas I got greater disapproval than I had anticipated, I relied more on my personal desire to advance in life. By the time I returned to the Director to give feedback, I had made my mind to accept the responsibility and I told him so.

Soon, I received posting instructions and full briefing about my assignment in the United Republic of Tanzania. I travelled to the country and embarked on the work. It was an uphill task, as some friends had foretold. I encountered various hurdles, some so acute that I might have rejected the offer if I had understood in time that they would occur.

Fortunately, they materialised when I was already in the country with limited chance to retreat. In the end, I met and exceeded all the targets. Pleased at my performance, the Head Office increased my benefits package and re-assigned me to the Republic of Malawi. There was nothing for me to fear, after all.

In the Sahara, the Tuareg people have a saying: "The courage of the water drop is to dare falling into the desert."

Courage is a gift from God whereas fear is a tool of the devil. A person who lives by fear is likely also to suffer from lack of the Holy Spirit.

St Paul emphasises to Timothy, "For God has not given us a spirit of fear and timidity, but of power, love, and self-discipline" (2 Timothy 1:7). Courage is therefore the evidence of God's Spirit in us and of our trust in him.

Addressing Ephesus, Paul further says, "... be strong in the Lord with his energy and strength. Put on the whole armour of God

... to resist the cunning of the devil" (Ephesians 6:10-11).

When you take a courageous step, you can achieve what unbelievers think is impossible

Scripture shows that David relied on courage and God's assurance to defeat Goliath and the entire Philistine armed forces. He was only a young boy who went to the battlefield carrying roasted grain and ten loaves for his brothers plus cheese for the field officer.

When he reached the combat zone, he noticed that one man, Goliath challenged the entire Israel army and they fled from him, terrified. David was concerned but when he expressed his intention to confront Goliath, his brother Eliab reminded him of his vulnerability.

In the words of Ralph Waldo Emerson, and American philosopher, essayist, poet and writer, "Whatever course you decide upon, there is always someone to tell you that you are wrong. There are always difficulties arising which tempt you to believe that your critics are right. To map out a course of action and follow it to an end requires ... courage."

David's known work was to look after the family sheep and Eliab blamed him for leaving the flock unattended. He was not expected to venture into the field of war and he was variously asked to sit down when he wanted to stand up.

David was seriously disadvantaged. First, he was very young. Second, he was not dressed for war. Third, he lacked experience and was untested in the art of war.

Even King Saul told him, "You cannot fight this Philistine for you are still young, whereas this warrior has been a warrior from his youth".

All the same, David went forward merely armed with a staff, five smooth stones and a sling to face Goliath who carried a sword, spear and javelin.

Goliath was disappointed to see that, of all people, a small, poorly armed boy aimed to challenge him and he cried out intimidatingly, "Come and I will give your flesh to the birds of the sky".

David shouted back, "I come against you with Yahweh.

The ultimate victor was David as he killed Goliath and the Philistine army fled in disarray (Samuel 17:17-45).

In a situation like this, Paul poses a key question, "…if God is with us, who shall be against us?" (Romans 8:31).

Harper Lee must have been right when she wrote, "I wanted you to see what real courage is, instead of getting the idea that courage is a man with a gun in his hand. (Courage is) when you know you're licked before you begin, but you begin anyway and see it through no matter what."[9]

To know that God is present in times of challenges is the basis for real courage. In the story of David and Goliath, the latter was powerful and courageous but he did not look to God for fortification; while the former was weak in almost every aspect but relied on God for success. The Israelites faced a myriad of risks on their trek from Egypt but Moses always referred to God for solutions.

During the Exodus, Moses told the Israelites, "Be courageous and strong, do not fear... God is with you; he will not leave you," (Deuteronomy 31:6-7).

---

9   Statement by Atticus Finch, a character in the novel, To Kill a Mockingbird, by Harper Lee (1960)

As time wore on, Moses had recognised that he would not be available to lead the Israelites into the Promised Land. He knew therefore that without him, they needed courage to get to their destination.

After the death of Moses, God urged his successor, Joshua, "Be valiant and have courage… be brave and faithfully fulfil the Law which Moses, my servant, gave you….Do not tremble or be afraid because…..your God is with you wherever you go," (Joshua 1:6-9).

While handing over the plans and tools for the construction of the Jerusalem temple, David assured Solomon that he would accomplish the task as long as he exhibited adequate courage.

He said, "Be strong, stand firm; be fearless, be determined and set to work because Yahweh….is with you. He will not fail you or abandon you…' (1 Chronicles 28:20).

What a grand task it was! How little Solomon knew about the original temple plan! How his courage, coupled with God's grace, was to be a stimulus to accomplish the task at hand!

Peter once desired to act like Jesus but he needed courage to do so. One day, Jesus was seen walking on water to the disbelief of his disciples. Taking clue from his leader, Peter mustered a little courage and tried to walk on water as well but he began to sink along the way. As he fought to avoid sinking, Jesus held him by the hand and pulled him to safety (Matthew 14:25-31).

By making a daring attempt at what seemed impossible, Peter must have been fulfilled though he got soaked in the process. Such is the joy of taking a courageous step. God is always available to save people who honestly undertake critical ventures in ways which unbelievers might consider risky.

William Shakespeare provides a beautiful piece about courage and cowardice. He writes:

> *Cowards die many times before their deaths.*
> *The valiant never taste of death but once.*
> *Of all the wonders that I yet have heard,*
> *It seems to me most strange that men should fear,*
> *Seeing that death, a necessary end,*
> *Will come when it will come.*[10]

---

10   William Shakespeare, Julius Caesar Act 2 Scene 2.

The gallant president of South Africa, Nelson Mandela writes in his autobiography, *A Long Walk to Freedom,* "I learned that courage was not the absence of fear, but the triumph over it. The brave man is not he who does not feel afraid, but he who conquers that fear."

Courage is bravery and it is a trait of strong character. It is the spirit and quality of mind that enables a person to face difficulty, danger or pain without fear. To have courage is to act in accordance with your beliefs regardless of criticism. The more we stand up, the firmer our convictions will be. The happier we will eventually be.

Christian history is coloured with countless saints and martyrs, who could not trade virtue for popularity or safety. St Thomas Moore forfeited his coveted office of Lord Chancellor as well as his life, but this has since become the bedrock of his reputation.

Robert Bolt (1966), in his book, 'A Man For All Seasons', cites Moore's words: "And when we die, and you are sent to heaven for doing your conscience, and I am sent to hell for not doing mine, will you come with me, for fellowship?"

Thomas Jefferson, the third president of the United States, must have been very right when he said, "One man with courage is a majority."

STAND OUT OF THE CROWD

A Proverb from Sierra Leone states, "If the cockroach wants to rule over the chicken, it must hire the fox as a bodyguard."

A fox guarding a cockroach would be a curious spectacle enough to draw everyone's attention. Likewise, you should be able to carve out a unique character by which you want to be known, if you desire to attain success.

Our world is full of corruption, violence, deceit, malice, adultery and all manner of mischief; so much that you can easily tell yourself that it is impossible, if necessary, to be different. It is said, sometimes, that 'no one is perfect', which almost implies that it is desirable to do 'a little wrong' sometimes. As a result, many people end up doing things they do not like in order to conform to the popular conduct of the society.

Leo Tolstoy (1882), in an essay, 'A Confession', counsels, "Wrong does not cease to be wrong because the majority share in it."

Wrongdoing may appear to be socially acceptable in many ways. A young girl might be tempted to lose her virginity if she learns that her peers have lost theirs. A public servant might be forced to steal office funds because all the colleagues in the department are doing the same.

A man might assault his wife if he learns that his peers in the community are always doing so. A business man might sell fake products to customers to be like others. Wicked conduct may appear as fashionable in giving quick advantage. However, you can stand out of the crowd by upholding what everyone else may be reluctant to promote.

I wanted to run away from my new job after two weeks because of discontent from many of my contemporaries. An international agency had appointed me as a communications officer on the programme for the prevention of the human immunodeficiency virus (HIV), locally known in Uganda as 'slim'.

The disease was spreading like a bush fire resulting into hundreds of thousands of new infections in the country every year. Shockingly, this was a familiar disease since the Ugandan public had known it for about thirty years. Nearly everyone knew its modes of transmission and methods of prevention but it remained a growing health hazard locally and globally.

Desperate situations demand desperate measures. Scientists advised the international community to start promoting male circumcision as an additional way to prevent the spread of the virus. They argued that scientific and observational research had yielded substantial evidence that circumcision significantly reduced a man's risk of acquiring *slim*.

Uganda received the findings with enthusiasm and started earnest preparations to promote male circumcision. My new job required me to lead the process for marketing the programme which was not merely new but obviously unpopular in the country. It was known largely as an Islamic tradition except in a few districts where it was a cultural rite.

As I signed the contract and reported for work, I had not heard about the stated relationship between male circumcision and *slim*. I only understood that my job involved communication about the usual prevention methods. It was proclaimed normally that unmarried people were required to abstain from sex or use condoms; those who intended to marry or already married were required to take medical tests together and stick to each other for sex, while people who were already infected with the virus were asked to get medication and avoid reinfection.

I was shocked to learn, on my first day at a new work place, that my job would involve promotion of male circumcision in Uganda. I was a practicing Christian. I came from a culture that despised people who did not have foreskins whether it was because of birth deformity, medical operation or cultural and religious rituals.

Although I was not comfortable with the issue that lay at the core of my job, I would never run away from a challenge so easily. I thus started to find ways of delivering the results. Yet I was concerned about the attitude people would have of me as an advocate for a suspicious agenda.

From time to time, I would smuggle the topic into casual conversations with other people to gauge the general mood towards male circumcision. I received coherent responses every day from everyone.

"You are killing your career," said an elder with whom I always shared secrets. "Look for another job to avoid looking funny before your friends," he advised.

Another person told me, "People will say you have converted to Islam! Even your church might condemn you!"

Someone even gave me a reasonable lecture, "Circumcision cannot prevent *Slim* because I know circumcised Muslims who have died of the disease. Even the tribes where every man is circumcised have people who have been infected. Therefore, you will not convince anyone."

One person who seemed to know the logic of male circumcision in reducing the spread of the virus did not see how the programme could succeed, nonetheless.

He said, "I have read about the research and I think it is authentic. But circumcision inflicts a wound on a man's core organ. I would rather abstain from sex forever than subject my precious tool to such a risk!"

Whether or not to embrace male circumcision as part of the HIV prevention strategy became very contentious. People exchanged opinions through articles published in newspapers, largely critical of this new technology. Callers into radio stations queried the motive of indorsing such an intervention in our country.

One day, a friend with whom I had studied at High School, and who graduated as a medical doctor thereafter, told me how he did not believe that male circumcision provided the health benefits that we had started to propagate.

"I am a doctor but I cannot get circumcised," he cried out, "because I'm not promiscuous. What you are telling people is nonsense!"

On my part, I saw the male circumcision programme as another opportunity to break new ground. Having overcome my initial fears, I read extensively about the subject and settled down to craft basic communication materials and relevant messages.

To popularise the innovation, I initiated numerous platforms such as public debates, media trainings, partners' meetings, social surveys, online updates, and radio programmes. Through these, pertinent stakeholders could contribute to the discussions on the advantages and demerits of male circumcision.

The trick worked. Demand for male circumcision grew by lips and bounds. In some locations, queues of circumcision candidates gradually became too long for the surgeons to clear within the fixed durations.

For the first time, the government instituted a national policy on male circumcision, along with a comprehensive communication strategy, with my input markedly embedded.

Scripture provides instructive cases of men and women who defied standard practice to uphold what their conscience valued. One such character was Noah, who lived in a society so perverted that the Lord regretted having created man (Genesis 6:6-7). While everyone else committed evil, Noah did not.

Noah was very aware of the popular behaviour of his contemporaries but he exercised restraint and remained blameless. He upheld his integrity and did not attempt to 'appear like others'.

It would have been very easy for Noah to say, "There is no one doing good so it will not hurt if I also do a little mischief."

It is said that when you are the only sane person in the community, people may see you as the only insane person. Noah chose right living while the rest of the world had elected wickedness.

He simply stood out. He alone remained righteous in a warped society. Other people may have viewed him as a 'social-misfit'. When the punitive flood wiped out everyone, however, Noah alone survived with his family.

The Lord said to Noah "Go into the ark; you and your household, for you... alone have I found righteous before me" (Genesis 6-7).

The Bible also offers a story of Job; a man who would not renounce his devotion to God at any cost. The people in his society sinned with reckless abandon in spite of the blessings God gave them. Yet, Job remained "a blameless and upright man who loved God and shunned evil" (Job 1:1).

Satan imagined that Job was cushioned from sin by the abundant wealth God had splashed on him. To challenge Noah's dignity, Satan visited on him such a volume of suffering that no other person could bear. All his ten children died along with his servants; all his animals perished and he became totally impoverished. He even got hurting sores all-over his body.

In his agony, Job got a lot of pressure from his companions, urging him to denounce God and submit to Satan's temptations. Even his wife asked him to curse God. Everyone around him knew that if they were in his situation, they would take any shortcut available, even if it were offered by the devil, as long as it would give them some relief. In his situation, however, Job only reacted by blessing God and praying for his friends who were exerting excessive pressure on him to capitulate.

In the end, God rewarded him, "Yahweh restored his fortunes, giving him twice as much as he had before…. Yahweh blessed Job's latter days with more than his earlier ones (Job 42:10-12).

Daniel is another biblical character who defied the odds. When he and his colleagues lived in captivity, they were given the chance to dine and wine from the table of Nebuchadnezzar, the king of Babylon. Daniel led his fellow youth to reject the offer so that they would not be soiled by unclean diet (Daniel 1:8).

Therefore, Daniel could not be compromised with cheap patronage. Whereas greed hardly brings lasting fulfilment, most people would easily sell their hearts for momentary relief, forgetting that challenges are the normal indicators of an impending windfall. For Daniel, a later king, Darius appointed him as a provincial governor whereupon he performed superbly and outshone all other administrators and satraps. The king planned to give him authority over the entire kingdom because he was so trustworthy that neither corruption nor negligence could be found in him.

Ordinarily, Daniel's peers became envious and plotted against him. They persuaded the king to kill him for his commitment to God. As a result, he was thrown into a den of lions which, they hoped, would devour him to death.

God would not allow that to happen. He sent an angel who closed the mouths of the lions and disabled them from harming Daniel. Not even a single injury was inflicted on him because "he had trusted in God" (Daniel 6:3-23).

The story of Daniel stresses the fact that the feeling of insecurity we get for challenging negative social tendencies is largely needless. It takes unusual courage to do what all other people are afraid of but this is the secret of success. When you are expected to be standing up, you should not sit down simply because everyone else is seated.

In his postcolonial novel, *Things Fall Apart*, the famous African writer, Chinua Achebe (1958) says, "The sun will shine on those who stand before it shines on those who kneel under them."

As an individual, one can inspire an entire community to face their challenges with confidence and ultimate success. Goliath was a giant among the Philistines and he alone gave their army a matchless reputation. He was feared more than his entire troops since he had possibly led them to several military victories.

When he issued a challenge, King Saul and all the soldiers "were afraid and greatly terrified" (1 Samuel 17:11).

One man with courage is a majority

The Bible, nevertheless, counsels, "Unless the Lord guards the city, the watchman keeps awake in vain" (Psalms 127:1).

Therefore, one must guard against becoming too opinionated to recognise God who is the guarantor of all the triumphs we crave for in life. When mighty Goliath made such a mistake, he succumbed to a mere pebble at the hands of a nascent boy, David.

While the Israeli forces cowered, David, immature as he was considered, was not overcome by collective fear. He stepped out to face the battle-hardened Goliath. He felled him with a sling and a stone, and the rest of the Philistine military took to their heels (1 Samuel 17:50-51). David stood out and achieved beyond everyone's expectation. Success remains elusive to people who fail to discover their personal strengths and tend to judge their chances by the attitude and behaviour of other members of their society.

This is why Zacchaeus would not miss the opportunity to see Jesus. Due to the crowds that surged around Jesus, Zacchaeus could only realise his dream by doing what no other person thought of. To stand out of the crowd, he ran ahead of others and climbed a sycamore tree. This was a creative approach and, as a result, he alone in Jericho got the chance to host Jesus Christ at his home (Luke 19:4-7).

No condition should stop a person from registering success.

Even if all the people in your society are failures, you should not have that as an excuse for becoming a failure as well. You owe it to yourself to make innovative choices and decisions. When you are determined about your mission, you can always lift yourself up from the dust of communal desolation.

As Max Lucado, an American clergyman once said, "A man who wants to lead the orchestra must turn his back on the crowd."

KNOW YOUR PRIORITIES

Someone said, "Success is only another form of failure if we forget what our priorities should be."

A priority is something which has greater importance than all others and, therefore, deserves to be given more attention.

It is something which must be done first, thus it is given the topmost place in the hierarchy of a person's choices. It is the most important concern that one must tackle before anything else.

An antelope will naturally run into the bush to avoid the hunter's bullet. However, it cannot stay in the hiding once the bush catches a fire. It will jump out, regardless of the risk of getting shot. The priority will be how to escape from the greater danger of being burnt alive. The antelope must choose one risk to take at all costs.

A young woman may get various suitors but must know what she wants in a man. Is it appearance? Money? Discipline? Brains? Parentage? Education? What else? While all these may be nice, she will go with the man who possesses the most desirable ideal in order to get a fulfilling marriage. If she cannot define her priorities, she is likely to enter a marriage she will never enjoy.

In 2010, I quit my job to contest for a Parliamentary seat in my home constituency, Kajara County. I lost due to obvious reasons. My decision to participate in the elections shocked many of my friends and acquaintances. It looked crazy that I could abandon a gainful contract to plunge into the murky politics of Uganda where depravity had reached obscene levels.

The consensus in offices and on social platforms was that any self-respecting person should not be associated with politicians who were clearly concerned about self-preservation other than serving the common good. The regime had entrenched an appalling culture which many decent persons believed should be ignored much as it was loathed since the political class seemed beyond redemption. Only God could resolve the situation at some point.

When I announced that I was offering myself for elections, therefore, some people believed I was taking a careless step. On a number of occasions, they advised me to reconsider my decision.

"It's true there is a lot of corruption. Our taxes are being abused. However, it's not only your money being stolen. The loss is suffered by all the citizens. Why do you want to make it a personal duty to tackle the problem?" someone challenged me.

"No matter how popular you may be, this government is famous for rigging elections," one friend pointed out, "therefore, don't waste your time contesting."

"You have a young family," another reminded me. "Why do you take a risk to oppose a government which, we all know, can harm you?"

Another asked, "We all know that the regime is mismanaging the country, but do you want to become a martyr?"

I had ever attended a rally, addressed by an opposition politician, where armed forces indiscriminately shot at people causing death and serious injuries. I had seen politicians arrested and incarcerated on trumped up charges for speaking in favour of justice and fairness. I had ever witnessed acts of intimidation by regime activists against people exercising their rights.

We had come to a level where theft was normal and glorified as a form of ingenuity. On the question of government officials stealing public funds while service delivery deteriorated, a friend counselled me, "Your family is benefitting from the medical insurance scheme. Your children are going to good schools. Poor service delivery, in the public sector, does not affect you directly. Leave π as π."

On the other hand, whenever I saw the suffering some people were going through, I always bled at heart even though I was not the exact victim. In the circumstances, therefore, something had to be done. Someone had to do it. I, too, had to make a contribution. It did not matter how comfortable I was, I believed that it was only a deceptive state: I was not safe if someone else was not.

During my secondary school days, I had learnt a compelling theory from East Africa's foremost author, Ngugi wa Thiong'o who, in a novel, *Petals of Blood* wrote, "Whenever any of us is degraded and humiliated, even the smallest child, we are all humiliated and degraded because it has got to do with human beings."

My priority in life is justice and human dignity. I hate oppression. I despise exploitation. I am appalled by cruelty. I love humanity. I adore God. I could sacrifice anything else for this reason.

Jesus said, "… a merchant looking for fine pearls… found one of great value… sold everything he had and bought it" (Matthew 13:45-46).

We have a lot of needs in life but the soul is the most important treasure everyone has and must toil to protect. Jesus calls it hollowness when a man pursues material things at the expense of the soul, which should be the priority.

"What good is it to gain the whole world while destroying your soul?" (Mark 8:36-37).

Saint Theresa said, "Remember that you have only one soul; that you have only one death to die; that you have only one life...If you do this, there will be many things about which you care nothing." Life demands making choices from among many goals a person has. A correct choice, a priority, automatically attracts other benefits to the person involved. Jesus Christ was an advocate of setting priorities and taught that the most important purpose of our existence is to know and worship the Creator who grants everything else we desire.

He said, "Seek the Kingdom of God above all else and He will give you everything you need" (Luke 12:31).

Martha and Mary had conflicting priorities when Jesus visited them at home. They had to entertain him with both food and a chat.

Martha used all her energy to make a meal while Mary just sat down to talk with the guest. Martha was sure that a guest had to get food as a priority, so she asked Jesus to rebuke Mary for evading work.

Instead, Jesus replied that Martha had got her priorities wrong, "… you worry and are troubled about many things, whereas only one thing is needed. Mary has chosen the better part" (Luke 10:41-42).

At one point, Jesus called a man to be his follower. The man was not ready to take the critical step to follow the Lord and, hence, looked for an excuse to dodge the responsibility. He said that whereas he was willing to follow Jesus, he wanted to return home and bury his father first. Jesus again faulted him for getting his priorities wrong.

He told him, "Follow me and let the dead bury their own dead..." (Matthew 8:22).

Scholars say that the man's father was not actually dead. He was not even bedridden with sickness. The man apparently meant that he wanted to stay with his father until he died, possibly several years later. Many people tend be preoccupied with petty affairs and, as a result, miss great opportunities which come looking like uncomfortable conditions. It takes a steady personality to recognise or set correct priorities.

The priority of a broody hen is not to hunt for food but to sit on her eggs.

Prophet Joshua had a chance to alert the Israelites against paying lip service to the worship of Yahweh. He proclaimed that the community had the choice to make God a priority in their lives or to relegate Him to the margins. Knowing the rightful place of the Lord, however, Joshua informed the Israelites that he would not adhere to the popular state of affairs.

He would lead his own family to serve God, "Now fear the Lord and serve him with all faithfulness.... But if serving the Lord seems undesirable to you... as for me and my household, we will serve the Lord...." (Joshua 24: 14-16).

Through Moses, God delivered Ten Commandments to the Israelites. Jesus Christ simplified the commandments when a Pharisee tried to test him with a question on whether any of the commandments was more important than others.

He used the moment to point out the priority commandment, "You shall love the Lord your God with all your heart, with all your soul and with all your mind. This is the first and the most important of the commandments" (Matthew 22:37-38).

Writing to the Christians, St. Paul emphasises that love is the finest virtue a person can have.

He said, "If I speak in the tongues of men or of angels…. If I have the gift of prophecy and can fathom all mysteries and all knowledge… if I have a faith that can move mountains…. If I give all I possess to the poor and give over my body… but do not have love, I am nothing" (1 Corinthians 1-3).

ALWAYS BE PATIENT

*"With a little patience, you will persuade the judge. A soft tongue can break bones" (**Proverbs 25:15**).*

When given options between short-term and long-term rewards, most people are inclined to choose the former.

This is mainly because people prefer to enjoy instant advantages and also they cannot be sure of getting the same advantage at a later stage. Yet, everyone knows that greater benefits tend to accrue from long-term investments, which explains why all successful investors are able to postpone enjoyment of their resources to a future time.

The secret to the realisation of any a dream is to have the time and courage to wait. A person who is patient does not easily get frustrated. Rather, he understands that an opportunity can only be delayed but it cannot be denied. It does not matter how long it may take to achieve a goal; a patient person will be able to wait without getting tired.

Someone recommended me to an organisation seeking to set up a communications unit, which required an innovative character. I secured the job soon after and started to work with usual enthusiasm. I was sure to deliver results as expected since I had done so several times earlier, including when I was still learning to work in a nongovernmental organisation.

I had logged into the website to acquaint myself with the profile of the organisation I was joining and found out that it was not only operating in my home country but also had branches elsewhere in the world. It was an international organisation and this excited me. My career was soaring further.

When I reported for work, however, I encountered setbacks that would make it almost impossible for me to fit in the establishment. The organisational culture was very different from what I knew. It was a slow-paced environment where everyone feared to make mistakes and, hence, there was limited room for innovation. On the other hand, I had hoped to boost the team with my expertise and thus lead to better project results.

The first staff meeting, attended by the Director, took place one month after I had joined the team. My supervisor had been observing me during this period and noticed that I was likely to run into problems due to my passion for quick results. He alerted me that I should pay full attention to the guidelines which the Director would communicate during the meeting and always act accordingly.

"Please, don't ask questions," he said, "because the Director might think that you are stubborn."

At the meeting, I watched the Director carefully but she looked very democratic. She beamed with smiles and gazed interestedly at each person during the introduction session. She nodded affirmatively to each person as they gave status reports about the work they had done.

When she talked, she praised the team for being hard working and challenged us to do even better. She welcomed me to the team and said she expected me to add value. She said that she wanted to hear more of the team members' thoughts and would be very glad to answer all their questions.

My supervisor was the first to speak and praised the Director for all the support to the team. He pointed out that, as usual, her communication was very clear and inspiring hence, he doubted that anyone had a question. He pledged, on behalf of every team member, that we were highly motivated to work even harder.

"She has said she would like to hear from us," I thought, "why is he saying nobody possibly has a question?"

I had been advised not to ask, so I did not although I needed clarification on a few issues. I decided I would get answers from my supervisor, later on. Whenever I asked, I found that only the Director could provide answers. Surprisingly, I always got negative feedback for any new idea that I advanced.

A believer in constructive engagement, I often tended to reply with a view to enrich the discussions and ultimately enhance the project performance. Little did I know that this was seen either as a sign of insubordination, contempt for institutional practice or being diversionary in order to evade duty!

My supervisor was not joking when he advised me to adhere to the Director's guidelines always. I had to learn the most important principle in the organisation: to follow instructions.

My previous employers had constantly stressed the importance of innovation at work and thus instilled in me a tendency to 'think out of the box'. I had almost forgotten that I was working in a new institution with a different culture.

As the English say, however, old habits die hard! Sometimes, I asked a challenging question, strongly defended a new concept, pointed out gaps in our work or changed an activity based on field realities.

The Director often reprimanded me and I got upset until I realised that I had to change my attitude. There was a bigger problem with my mind-set than with the system I was operating in. It was not important to get upset; the essential thing was to deliver results.

While I got upset, I also understood that I did not get the job as a punishment. I had freely signed the job contract. I had an opportunity to resign but that meant I would leave the organisation without delivering significant results. It would show that I did not only fail to do the work but also that I could not adjust to the new situation.

I believed that I had to spend a few years in the organisation for me to make a meaningful contribution. When I took up another job three years later, I was happy to note that a lot of what I had done, including what I had been rebuked for, was highly appreciated and approved for my successors to maintain. My patience was not in vain!

In the parable of the sower, Jesus Christ demonstrates that, in some situations, patience is the only option we have in order to get results, while impatience could be deceptive. The seeds that fell on the rock germinated quickly but withered easily due to lack of moisture. Seeds that fell among the thorns grew very fast in competition for light but were easily choked by the stronger plants. On the other hand, "… some seeds fell on good soil and grew, producing fruit, a hundred times as much. The good soil, instead, are people who receive the word and keep it in a gentle and generous mind and, preserving patiently, they bear fruit" (Luke 8:5-15).

According to St. Augustine, 'patience is the companion of wisdom'. It is the ability to accept delay without getting upset. It means waiting without complaining. Most people desire and work for success but are not willing to wait for it.

A Chinese proverb states, "Man fools himself: he prays for a long life but he fears old age."

See how the sower awaits for the precious fruits of the earth, looking forward patiently

Our society manifests impatience in many ways. In a restaurant, an impatient client finds it easy to yell at the attendant other than waiting patiently to be served or walking to the next one where the services may be faster. An impatient road user will violate traffic rules by driving on the pavement, overtaking at a red spot, hooting without cause or ignoring traffic lights.

In other cases, someone may become rude to others such as family members, work mates, friends and customers. An impatient worker will easily resign a job before identifying any other employment opportunities.

As a popular saying teaches, "Only a fool will break a door when someone has agreed to open it."

Every person has needs and, the faster they are satisfied, the better. You may present your petitions to God but you do not have to put deadlines. God does not act on deadlines. Man must wait on the timing of God - for both physical and spiritual benefits.

To emphasise the value of patience, an African proverb states, "At the bottom of patience, one finds heaven."

Impatient people tend to be stressed and frustrated when they pursue their goals and find some delays along the way. As a result, they give up easily. Scripture shows that when we put our trust in God, we cannot get frustrated in our pursuit of success.

"Those who hope in Yahweh will renew their strength. They will soar as with eagle's wings. They will run and not grow weary; they will walk and never tire" (Isaiah 40:31).

When an impatient individual gives up, they provide sufficient space for others who are able to be patient. The competition for limited opportunities therefore reduces.

The Moroccans, in a proverb, say, "There is no crowding at the gate of patience."

St. Peter also says, "The Lord is not slow to fulfil his promise as some count slowness, but is patient toward you…" (2 Peter 3:9).

To give up is to lose confidence in oneself and also in God. St Paul says that God does not disappoint but his blessings are realized by those who are not looking for instant rewards but ones who are able to wait with hope. "So we hope for what we do not see and we will receive it through patient hope" (Romans 8:25).

A person who is sure that he has made a good decision should be confident and firm in whatever he does. Writing to the Galatians, St Paul urged them to be steadfast in everything good they did. He advised them to ignore anything that might seem to upset their determination to succeed. St. Paul counsels, "Let us not become tired of doing good, for at the proper time, we shall reap our harvest, if we do not give up" (Galatians 6:9). In the garden of Gethsemane, Jesus Christ noticed that human beings were weak and could not endure laborious moments. He understood that our nature makes it hard for us to remain firm amidst challenges. Many people easily break down when they meet obstacles while pursuing their goals, whereas patience would make it easy for them to register success.

As he prayed, Jesus returned thrice where the apostles were and found them asleep each time "…because their eyes were heavy." He told them that 'prayer' was the only trick they could use to remain strong.

He said, "Watch and pray so that you will not fall into temptation. The spirit is willing but the body is weak" (Luke 22:43). In life, success sometimes comes directly as anticipated.

However, we should also be ready to wait for some time if it delays. "Be patient …. See how the sower waits for the precious fruits of the earth, looking forward patiently.… You also be patient and do not lose heart…" (James 5:7-8).

Every person has a lot things to do in a day, week, month and year or in life; yet it is impossible to get enough time, energy and other resources to enable us do everything. It is inevitable, therefore, that many things are left undone, no matter how hard one tries. It is unwise to tackle the least desirable issues at the cost of the most important matters. The only solution is to set priorities.

RUN FOR SUCCESS

"If racing against mere men makes you tired, how will you race against horses?" (Jeremiah 12:5).

During the Rotary Cancer Run (2014), I rolled up to Kololo airstrip ready to race in the Ten-kilometre category. There were quite a number of athletic young men and girls but I was stirred particularly by the participation of so many elderly men and women, bulky women, young children and people with disabilities.

As the race was flagged off, I marked out a tall, thin ageing man who seemed bored about the activity at hand and generally less excited about life. I told myself that if all the other runners proved to be faster than I would be, I should ensure that I finished the race ahead of this dismal participant. I had been concerned about the possibility of coming last in the race, but from the time I saw the elderly racer, I became sure that I would beat someone.

The chief runner, Rais Mstafu Ali Hassan Mwinyi, the former President of the United Republic of Tanzania, stout but aged, soon commanded us to start running. Everyone in the crowd struggled to run but there was no sufficient space. Therefore we all set off in a walking mode. We gathered speed gradually as we covered scores of metres away from the starting point.

About four hundred metres away, I found that I was running ahead of more people than I was following. I began to believe that if I increased my pace, I could emerge winner of the race or possibly be recognised among the leading participants. Scripture says, "… they who wait for the Lord shall … run and not be weary; they shall walk and not faint (Isaiah 40:31).

I struggled and panted along, outpacing more and more people, as others who had been far behind gradually also caught up and overtook me. To my shock and dismay, I looked ahead of me and noticed the 'tall, thin ageing man' whom I had targeted to beat. He was jogging at a comfortable pace.

I revived my intention to defeat him at all costs. However, just like a hunting dog running faster than the hunter, the man progressively increased the distance between him and me before he eventually disappeared from my sight.

I would not give up though since the Bible counsels, "… let us also lay aside every weight… let us run with endurance the race that is set before us (Hebrews 12:1).

We successfully went through the winding roads and returned to Kololo amidst gasps and half-breaths. The noise that had marked the start of the race was unmistakeably absent. Few participants, including this writer, cared to find out what position they had earned in the running competition. They apparently drew fulfilment from the fact that they entered and completed the race. At Kololo, everyone walked about the pitch to find out if there were others they knew who had participated in the race. People congratulated others, narrated their varied experiences and generally promised to return should another chance to run ever appear.

Like Paul, everyone seemed to say, "I have fought the good fight, I have finished the race, I have kept the faith" (2 Timothy 4:7). Such is the joy we derive from working hard in pursuit of excellence and success. By declaring, "I have finished the race," Paul implies that he had put every effort into the work of proclaiming the gospel of salvation. He had completed the course set before him. He had done everything in his means; thus ready to cross the finish line into heaven.

In the case of the Rotary Cancer Run, some people came out first. Indeed, a few participants were crowned with awards for exceptional performance. Some people finished close to the winners but did not receive prizes - and I believe I was one of them. Others actually came last! On my way home, I saw some people walking towards the finishing line long after the entire ceremony had ended. It is just my considered view, however, that all the runners were winners. By virtue of participation, the racer who came off as the very last performed much better than all the people who did not show up for challenge, regardless of their likelihood to display greater speed if they had participated.

What mattered to most people was not to win the race; rather they were delighted to participate. Indeed, individuals who were singled out as winners were so excited; they too had been pleased to compete without assurance that they would win. Their triumph came largely as a surprise. To win the race, therefore, one had to participate in the running but since the organisers could only crown a few participants as winners, to get the accolade was another matter.

"…in a race, all the runners run but only one receives the prize…" (1 Corinthians 9:24).

The fundamental thing was to play a part, which demonstrated one's good will towards the cause for which the race was organised. People always run with a purpose: either chasing something good or fleeing from something dangerous.

Life is a race. You are either chasing opportunities or escaping from danger

People who do not run are can never succeed in life because they neither pursue their desires nor escape from their limitations. Life is a race and every person who wishes to enjoy success must run. There are countless opportunities towards which you must run. This is the only thing required of you. In the same vein, there are a myriad of problems from which you should run to improve your status. "Never pray to be a better slave when God is trying to get you out of your situation."

Writing in the *Sunday Vision* edition of 21 September 2014, Mr Sam Bwaya who ranked himself as having finished last in the Rotary Cancer Run said, "I was pretty sure that my legs were begging me to pull out of the race…. 'You man, put in more effort. Your friends have already arrived at Kololo,' shouted one bystander. A few others jeered at me…. It is funny how spectators think they can do better than people on the field…."

Sam went on, "I dug deep and from somewhere came some energy. I felt my legs could move again…. A few people around me started clapping and then, as if I was outside my body, saw myself cross the line…. They caught me before I collapsed and took me to the Red Cross tent for first aid."

The people who arrested Jesus Christ at Gethsemane also attempted to punish a curious young man who was at the scene, scantily dressed. Instead of submitting to the cruelty of the violent mob, the young man abandoned his artless garment and escaped totally undressed.

"And a young man followed him, with nothing but a linen cloth about his body. And they seized him, but he left the linen cloth and ran away naked" (Mark 14:51-52)

At the time of the Exodus, the Israelites had to run out of Egypt in order to escape slavery. The king of Egypt was told that the Israelites had 'fled' (Exodus 14:5). To 'flee' is to 'run away'. Running is so important that we cannot laugh at the man or woman who comes last during the race, as long as they ran. To become the fastest runner is good but it is not the only thing needful.

The fastest runner is not necessarily always the winner. The winner is he who knows what to do after completing the race.

When Peter and John heard that Jesus had resurrected, they went there to confirm.

"Both of them were running… but John outran Peter and reached the tomb first…. Then Peter came… and went into the tomb…" (John 20:3-6). Both John and Peter performed very well and won at different levels: John is known for getting to the tomb ahead of Peter; while Peter is recognised for entering the tomb ahead of John. One race; two winners; different ways!

PRAY TO FORTIFY YOUR CONFIDENCE

"Prayer is the key of the morning and the bolt of the evening," says Mahatma Gandhi, the pre-eminent leader of the Indian independence movement.

His counterpart, A.P.J. Abdul Kalam the eleventh President of India, is also known to have stated, "God, our Creator, has stored within our minds and personalities, great potential, strength and ability. Prayer helps us tap and develop these powers." Prayer can be compared to the extraction of a precious mineral from deep inside the soul to the surface in order to make it available and usable to the person and his community for their wellbeing. It is the person's submission to the Divine identity to generate success. By praying frequently, you go beyond your limited ability to attain a higher capability. All human effort, therefore, must be buttressed by Devine Providence to yield meaningful outcomes.

Jesus Christ says, "Ask and it will be given to you; seek and you will find; knock and the door will be opened to you… everyone who asks receives; the one who seeks finds; and to the one who knocks, the door will be opened" (Matthew 7:7-8).

To pray is, ideally, to request God to grant us good things. At times, however, Nyabo offered alarming prayers. Instead of praying for wealth, health or love, she would dedicate a whole prayer session to unpopular themes like contentment in times of scarcity and joy amidst poverty. She would pray for the grace to bless our enemies, faithfulness amidst suffering, tolerating sickness as a way of sharing the cross of Jesus, giving up our pleasures for the sake others, and accepting death without protest.

Surprisingly, Nyabo was a member of the church army, known as the Legion. This was a movement of religious combatants: God's Army. They believed that in the spiritual warfare, the only armament needed was prayer.

In the family, Nyabo taught us that during prayers, the entire community of God comes together as a combined force which is able to triumph over the evil one. This force, she said, included individuals on earth, angels and saints in heaven and the Trinity. Therefore, our family rarely missed prayers in the morning, evening and at mealtime.

We would pray not only for ourselves but also for the sick, travellers, refugees, the hungry and even the dead. Nyabo insisted on adherence to all church guidelines such as mandatory Sunday attendance, regular Holy Communion, and constant penitence. She had learnt that prayers could move mountains and the only thing one needed was faith for one's prayers to be answered.

She taught the family that there should never a moment of hopelessness for a Christian. When I got drafted in school, Nyabo had sent me to church for basic catechism lessons. At the age of eleven, I was obviously too old to start school but she told me that with God, nothing was impossible.

I was the lastborn and all my siblings had dropped out school, to Sebo's disappointment. It was nearly obvious that the family would never attain redemption through education. Suddenly, the catechist behaved in the most unusual manner and forced us into school. I was able to complete school in Nyabo's lifetime.

Looking back, I feel that this was God's way of answering Nyabo's prayers. The family was poor but managed to raise money for my education, although in the hard way. Sebo was always in debt but never lost property to the debtors, unlike his peers.

In Nyabo's old age, the family had recovered from abject poverty. She also always prayed for a decent death and God granted it. One day, she complained of mysterious pains before she was rushed for treatment. Lying on a hospital bed, she died peacefully at the age of eighty.

God is integral of every personality, which means you can achieve anything you want if you recognise and fully apply your God-given potential.

Man is a mixture of earthly substance and Divine character; therefore, it is necessary to evoke the internal divinity in whatever one does in order to achieve one's goals. The natural way to express our Divine character is through prayer. In one of his sermons, Englishman Frederick Brotherton Meyer, a Baptist pastor, evangelist and author taught that the greatest tragedy is not prayers which God does not answer to, but prayers which are not offered to Him.

To pray is to go beyond your personal life to tap into the God within. God created man in His image and gave him life by puffing His own breath into him (Genesis 2:7). In this way, God infused Himself with man and is the cause of all human success.

Jesus Christ compares the unity of God and man with the bond between a tree and branch. "No branch can produce fruits by itself; it must remain on the vine…. I am the vine; you are the branches… (John 5:4-5). In the same spirit, Jesus Christ gives instructions on how to keep the God-man bond unbroken, "Whoever eats my flesh and drinks my blood, lives in me and I in him (John 6:56).

Through Holy Communion, a Christian is able to receive the flesh and blood of Jesus Christ; therefore, the Eucharist is the best way to replenish the Divine presence within.

Prayer is the acknowledgement of God's participation in our private and public affairs and, since nothing is impossible for Him, we are always sure to register success through prayers. By praying, we express confidence in the infinite power of our Creator to pay attention to our needs and desires.

As Richard Trench, a poet and Anglican Archbishop of Dublin (1864-1884) once said, prayer is not about getting man's will done in heaven; instead, it is about getting God's will done on earth. By prayer, we invite God into our earthly affairs to provide for our earthly needs and ultimately enable us to attain the heavenly splendour.

The chief element in prayer is "confidence" which may also be referred to as faith or trust. It may be described as 'the will'; a person's inner drive to commit resources in terms of possessions, time, mind and body to get results. One who prays demonstrates his desire and determination to sweat and secure success.

God does not sweat to grant a person's wishes since, as nineteenth century Danish philosopher, Søren Kierkegaard says, "Prayer does not change God; it changes him who prays'.

Prayer therefore demands a deliberate effort to interact with God for the benefit of the supplicant.

Failure to pray is failure to summon the inner potential to the fore and, thus, subjecting the spiritual element to the physical being. When you allow your human character to dominate the Divine identity within, your propensity to pray becomes suppressed, along with it, your sacredness. Jesus Christ encouraged people to pray always, but also lamented that many are too weak to pray adequately.

He said, "Stay awake and pray all of you…. The spirit is willing but the body is weak" (Mark 14:38).

In Gethsemane, the disciples were overcome by drowsiness. Jesus wished they could stay alert to witness his final moments before crucifixion. At heart, the disciples desired to continue interacting with him but were physically pooped and tended to sleep. Although Jesus understood their human weakness, he advised them not merely to be strong and remain awake but mainly to pray.

To pray is to prove that God is with us

In the words of Dwight Lyman Moody, an American evangelist, publisher and founder of the Moody Church, "Every great movement of God can be traced to a kneeling figure."

Prayer is a conversation with God; therefore, it should not be a monologue where God is reduced to a listening post. A good conversation involves speaking and listening; an interactive exchange of views. To have a fruitful dialogue with God, you should be able to do two things simultaneously; talk to Him but also listen to Him for the obligations he assigns you.

Arthur Tappan Pierson, in his work, *George Müller of Bristol and His Witness to a Prayer-hearing God*, describes how we interact with God during prayer, " We are to argue our case with God, not indeed to convince Him, but to convince ourselves…… we demonstrate to our own faith that He has given us the right to ask and claim, and that He will answer our plea…"

When you pray with sincerity, you earn God's grace to achieve anything that you would otherwise have not been able to accomplish. To obtain answers to our prayers, there are standards to uphold.

St. James says, "…you do not get what you want because you do not pray for it. You pray for something and do not get it because you pray with the wrong motive…" (James 4:2-3). For God to listen to your prayers, repent your sins first and bear no malice at heart; as Jesus Christ says, "… if you stand to pray…forgive, so that your heavenly Father may also forgive your sins (Mark 11:24-26).

When you pray, do not give God deadlines. He knows the best time to answer your prayers. In his heydays, Zechariah prayed for a son but only got the answer when he was very old.

He was utterly surprised when the angel told him, "…be assured that your prayer has been heard… your wife will bear a son" (Luke 1:13-14).

The couple were no longer anticipating the fulfilment of their desire for a child; they were resigned to die childless. Zechariah was no longer expectant of any answers to his prayers.

Expressing his disbelief, he asserted, "I am an old man and my wife is advanced in years" (Luke 1:18).

Prayer therefore demands patience and hope. "With a little patience, you will persuade the judge… (Proverbs 25:15).

Prayer also demands effort. Hannah was childless unlike Penninah, her co-wife who irritated her so much that she always wept and failed to eat. While in the temple, Hannah was so consumed in prayer that the priest thought she was drunk. She prayed so hard that she was able to give birth to a son, Samuel (Samuel 1:11).

Hannah's conduct shows that prayer requires full attention. Prayer time should be quality time, without necessarily being too long and wordy.

"When you pray, do not use a lot words as the pagans do…. Your Father knows what you need even before you ask him" (Matthew 6:7-8).

This means also that you should be organised when you pray.

Be consistent with prayer. Do not pray when in need, only to forget when you are in good times.

"Pray continually and do not lose heart" (Luke 18:1).

You must also have faith when you pray. Whatever you ask for in prayer, believe that you have received it, and it shall be done for you (Mark 11:24). God answers prayers which are offered with faith. God is part of your life. "…you are God's temple…the Spirit abides within you…God's temple is holy and you are this temple" (1 Corinthians 3:16-17).

When you pray, you summon the self-confidence and self- belief within and you inspire yourself as the major agent for causing success in your life.